LUCKY BREAK?

Graham Hurley

*Neil Slatter broke his neck in a motor cycle
accident. He was 19. For the rest of his life he
would be paralysed from the shoulders down.
Yet four years later he says he's the luckiest man
in the world. Why?*

Milestone Publications
Project Icarus

Published by Milestone Publications
Murray Road, Horndean, Hampshire PO8 9JL.

ISBN 0 903852 35 7

Design: Brian Iles
Photography: John King

Printed and bound in Great Britain by
R.J. Acford, Chichester, Sussex.

in conjunction with
Project Icarus
Raglan House,
4 Clarence Parade,
Southsea, Hampshire PO5 3NU.

Contents

To Eileen, Neil's Mum

Foreword

Because of my position as manager of a top football club, I do lots of charity appearances — and I must have met literally thousands of handicapped kids. But this is the first time I've ever appreciated what it really means to be paralysed. Here is a perfectly normal lad. He's young, he's fit, he's got the world at his feet. We get lots of them tapping at the doors of the club. Then he falls off his motorbike and breaks his neck.....and suddenly he's paralysed and having to face up to all those questions we never really think about. How's he going to eat? Shave? Pee? Make love? How's his girlfriend going to react? How will his family cope? Will he ever get a job again? Neil had no choice except to confront those questions, and the book is a remarkable tribute — both to the lad himself, and to all the people who made it possible for him to face life again. Sure, in physical terms Neil's only half the man he was but in my book he gets more out of life than most of us. He's seen the worst, and he's come through it all, and he's still in there punching. Able-bodied people who complain about life should be ashamed of themselves, reading about a lad like him.

Lawrie McMenemy
Manager
Southampton F.C.

The Author

Graham Hurley, 36, was born at Clacton-on-Sea, Essex, and educated at Forest School, London, and Cambridge University. He's worked as a television producer for eleven years, and a number of his documentary films have won international awards. He's written several novels, and a series of thrillers for Australian television. His film profile of Neil Slatter was transmitted on British Independent Television in 1981; his documentary report on the latest advances in spinal injury research — "THE CURE?" — was transmitted on Channel Four in 1982.

NOTE ON PROJECT ICARUS:

Project Icarus is a small charity company based in Southsea, Hants. Run on a part-time, unpaid basis by five friends, it produces health education material for schools, youth groups, colleges, and other interested organisations. A number of Project Icarus film documentaries have won international awards and are in regular use world wide. These include "Better Dead?", the most widely used British film on drug abuse ever made. Project Icarus poster sets on subjects ranging from alcoholism to birth control have also been praised for their impact and originality. LUCKY BREAK? is Project Icarus's first venture into publishing, and is intended to be one of a series of studies of lives in crisis.

Acknowledgements

Books like this don't get written without the trust and patience of a great number of people. To Neil, of course, it owes everything. He was never quite sure where it was going, but en route we had some very good evenings. To me, this new friendship is at least as important as the book itself. Toni, too, was marvellous. I think she had a shrewd idea where it all might lead, but she never missed a single meeting. Eileen and Bob, Neil's Mum and Dad, were more than generous with their time — as were Neil's brothers, Graham and Robert. To both sets of wives, I apologise for the nights on the ale. Keith Wilde and Jan Heidecker also entrusted me with a great deal of time and information. To them, as well, my thanks.

Outside the immediate circle of Neil's family and friends, I spent many hours in the various worlds around which this story revolves. At Stoke Mandeville, I got more time than I deserved from Sister Marion Rose, and from various helpful individuals in the X-Ray, Physio, and Occupational Therapy Departments.

Mr. John Russell, Director of the new Odstock Spinal Injuries Unit, was kind enough to vet the medical aspects of the book, and to him — as well — I'd like to extend my thanks. David Glanz of the Portsmouth 'News', Jane Mercer of Hampshire Social Services, Clare McKenna of the same organisation and David Hooper of the East Hants District Council were all tremendously helpful. The same goes for Mary Hopcroft of the South East Hants Care Attendance Scheme, and Inspector Batley and PC Alec Budd of the Surrey Constabulary.

Jack Boxall and Frank Dominie of the Surrey Ambulance Service devoted an afternoon to recounting some remarkable memories, and Mr. Anwar Chaudhri, an orthopaedic specialist at the Royal Surrey County Hospital, got up earlier than I thought possible to spare me a little of his hard won time. Stephen Bradshaw, of the Spinal Injuries Association, gave me mountains of research material and ran an old campaigner's eye over the final draft.

The staff at the Red Lion Hotel in Petersfield provided the friendliest of settings for a great deal of intimate conversation and Lynda Dare typed the final manuscript with a deft touch and a rare turn of speed. John King took the photographs and did a lovely job.

Finally, there's my wife Jane. She's lived with the clack of the Olivetti far too long to have any misconceptions about the glamour of authorship. For the long haul, my apologies. For the endless cups of tea, my grateful thanks. For everything else, my love.

4 February 1983
Southsea, Hants.

Prelude

Had there been any witnesses, it would have looked the silliest accident. For one thing, the road was empty and dry. There was no traffic, no sharp bends, no wet leaves, no oil slicks, no sudden obstructions. Just a glorious July day on a gentle stretch of country road between the Surrey town of Hindhead and the nearby village of Churt.

The motor bike was on the small side: a blue Honda 175cc CD. Driving it was a youth of nineteen called Neil Slatter. He was six feet tall, broadly built, wore a plaid shirt, denim jacket, jeans and boots. On the back was a friend called Tim: slightly older, slightly bigger, nursing a bag of groceries from a shopping expedition to the local store a mile up the road.

The bike slowed for a series of gentle bends. Neil later estimated his speed at "not more than thirty-five". Then, abruptly, he felt the balance of the bike change. He began to look round, half sensing that Tim had fallen off, but already the bike was out of control. "It just went on without me...." he said, "... as if I'd collided with some kind of invisible wall."

Neil hit the road with a bang, the back of his head against the warm tarmac. The force of the impact drove the breath from his body and when he opened his eyes there was nothing, just blackness and a faraway whistling in his ears. Mentally he tried to take stock, to check what hurt and where and how badly, but in the darkness it was hard to come to conclusions. The bike had gone, and his shopping with it, and here he was flat on his back wondering why.

Slowly sensation returned, and with it a sharp pain where his right hand had scraped along the road. Still in total darkness, he flexed it. Where the nail on his little finger had punctured the flesh on the next finger, it hurt even more. He tried blinking but nothing happened. Whatever he did with his eyes, the darkness wouldn't go away. Confusion gave way to fear. He began to panic.

Next came the noises. He couldn't be certain, but it sounded like a bus. The bus stopped. There were footsteps, a woman's voice, then a sudden weight on his chest. He gasped, tried to talk, but the voice above him was insistent. "Don't move" it said, "Whatever you do, don't move". Then the weight had gone again, and with it the voice. Only the darkness remained.

Some time later, seconds perhaps, or minutes, or even longer, there were more voices, the sound of car doors, footsteps, people running. He lifted his arms to his head and found his helmet wedged over his face. "Get it off..." he pleaded, "... get it off me... I can't breath..." Some one knelt beside him, asking him if he was OK and he said yes, get the helmet off, please get the helmet off, the words muffled by the shattered polycarbonate. Then there were hands at his head, easing the remains of the helmet back over his face, letting in the daylight and the fresh air. "It was extraordinary..." he said later, "... all the pain just suddenly went. Everything. It was as if someone had turned it off like a tap. It was like having gas at the dentist. One minute it all hurt like hell. And the next minute there was nothing, just peace, it was incredible..."

It was exactly at this moment, mid-afternoon on a country road in Surrey, that Neil Slatter's broken neck began to turn into paralysis.

Chapter One

Droxford is a small, pretty village in Hampshire's Meon Valley. Northward, the road winds up through a succession of similar villages towards Alton, while to the south lies the busy conurbation of Portsmouth, Fareham and Southampton. As a pleasant, peaceful spot to live, Droxford is much favoured by retired admirals, young professional couples, and local farming folk. It has a church, two pubs, a few shops and a small estate of council houses. One of these became home to the Slatter family in February 1953. Six years later the third and youngest son was born. His name was Neil. The date, appropriately enough, was Friday 13th June.

The Slatters were a close, busy family. Neil's father, Bob, is a short, square, thickset man, with large hands and a look of permanent anxiety. His war service took him to the Merchant Navy, and after his ship was torpedoed he spent seven hours floating unconscious in the Atlantic off Sierra Leone. After the war he went into forestry and became a tree feller, leaving Droxford every morning to work in the surrounding woodlands. The work was well-paid, but tough, yet Bob still found the time and energy to cope with the local Scout troop.

Bob's wife, Eileen, shared his appetite for a full life. A small, determined, cheerful woman, she managed to combine the demands of three sons with a job in the local primary school. In the evenings she also ran the cub pack and helped out with the local amateur dramatic group. The workload sounds daunting, if not impossible, but looking back she has only the fondest memories. Her life revolved around her three sons, and whatever they did, she did. Thus the school job, and the cub pack and Bob's Scout work, and perhaps even the amateur dramatics. "We were a real family" she says, "We were always on the go, but we were very, very close".

Both Neil's older brothers went to the local secondary school at nearby Swanmore before finding jobs. Graham, ten years older than

1

Neil, did a course as a dental technician before settling for a profitable career as a central heating engineer; and Robert, seven years older than Neil, moved on to Bromley Technical College and there did an electrical engineering course. The age gap between Neil and his brothers is probably important because Robert was already seven by the time Neil was born, and to some extent Neil therefore had his mother to himself. Certainly they became very close. Neil had been conceived as a possible substitute for their first child, a daughter, who'd died — and even now he occasionally views his name as a hasty adaptation of 'Nellie'.

But whatever his mother's prior wishes, Neil grew up as an exuberant, outgoing, utterly normal young boy. Eileen remembers him as "... forward and very confident... always into everything... always in the lead... always determined to see things through... if something was going on, you could be sure that Neil was in the thick of it..." From time to time Eileen has been accused of spoiling Neil, of turning him into a mother's boy, but this she denies. "If anyone was spoiled it was Graham" she says, "He was the one who was always so shy and inward looking. Neil never had any problems that way".

But problems there were. When he was eight, Neil earned himself an early taste of hospital life after an accident with a golf club. Rushed by ambulance to Winchester Hospital, he remained semi-conscious for a week while doctors fought to save the sight of his left eye. The operations were finally successful but Neil was obliged to stay in hospital for a long period of convalescence. He was by no means a model patient, and his mother made twice daily journeys to the hospital to get him up and put him to bed. The twenty-four mile round trip took several hours by bus and Eileen has vivid memories of the way her infant son would sit out on the balcony for hours, watching for his mother to arrive. "It was heartbreaking..." she says, "...there'd be this little figure in the dressing gown up there on the balcony just waiting. And once I'd arrived he'd steal things from my handbag and hide them down his bed, just to make sure I stayed. He used to make a dreadful fuss".

Neil remembers little of this incident except the company of his favourite teddy bear, Pooh. Pooh had accompanied him to Winchester in the back of the family Morris and had later been honoured with an X-Ray, appearing on the smoky photographic negatives as a patch of nose and a pair of button eyes.

Back home after the accident, Neil returned to his class at Droxford Primary. From there he was set to follow in his brother's footsteps to

Swanmore Secondary, but once again circumstances intervened. This time it was Bob's turn.

Bob's job had by this time taken him to the Queen Elizabeth Forest, a relatively new plantation on the steep chalk uplands south of Petersfield. Bob normally worked with a mate called Dick, and one cold morning found them felling a large beech tree deep in the forest. Between them, over the years, they'd developed what they both regarded as a fail-safe system for dropping the big beeches, but on this particular morning the system went disastrously wrong. Dick either misunderstood or didn't hear Bob's shout of warning and the 15-ton trunk crushed him as it fell. Bob ran headlong down the hill to pull his mate to safety, but when he finally reached him it was obvious he'd been killed instantly.

Over the subsequent weeks and months Bob was haunted by the accident. The Coroner's Court cleared him of any blame but the fact was that his mate had died as a direct consequence of Bob's work, and that knowledge he found almost impossible to live with. Deeply troubled, his confidence took a further knock when another felling accident with a chain saw landed him in hospital, and at this point he and Eileen began to think in terms of a change of occupation. There then followed a succession of jobs before Eileen noticed a joint husband and wife post advertised at Bedales, a boarding school with a progressive reputation, at Steep, near Petersfield. The job would employ Bob as a caretaker, and Eileen as a domestic and although the money was less than half his earnings with the forestry, the school were offering accommodation in the shape of a cottage on the estate. After some discussion, the Slatters decided to leave Droxford and start anew.

For Neil, it was his first-ever change of surroundings. "The cottage wasn't at all like Droxford. The whole place was painted orange. Dad was always sawing and hammering and slapping on coats and coats of new paint. It totally absorbed him, which I suppose is why he did it. I guess it saved him from thinking too hard about the trees".

By this time, Neil was eleven, one term away from leaving primary school for secondary school. Accordingly, he spent that final term at the local Steep primary school before transferring to the nearest secondary school which was at Petersfield. Both his brothers had by now left school, but Neil had formed a particularly close attachment to Robert, seven years older. It was Robert who passed on a passion for guitar music, and over the next half dozen years it was from Robert that Neil was to pick up a number of other interests, some of them permanent, some of them transitory. Neil's father, Bob, described the relationship in terms of hero-worship. "For Neil..." he says, "...Robert could do no wrong".

Over the next few years, Neil shouldered his way through adolescence with a deft step and a marked sense of self-confidence. At school he was popular, forceful and academically above average. He excelled at maths, technical drawing and engineering. On the sportsfield, he enjoyed rugby — and his prowess at swimming was established in front of an astonished family on the occasion of a sponsored swim. Prior to the event, Neil had asked his father for sponsorship and Bob had taken a precautionary look at his son in action before deciding on the sum per length. Neil's display was far from impressive and Bob therefore pledged a generous 2/6d. per length. But when the sponsored swim actually took place, Neil staged an abrupt and somewhat phoney improvement to complete at least twenty lengths, leaving Bob two pounds ten shillings the poorer. It was, announced Neil, all for a deserving cause.

Out of school, Neil could be equally canny. Eileen, ever keen to stay in touch with her offspring, encouraged Neil to bring his friends home. The cottage on the Bedales Estate, though, was far from spacious, and Neil's favourite haunt quickly became an ancient caravan which was parked outside in the garden. It was here that Keith Wilde, a newcomer to Steep, first met him. At fourteen, he was the same age as Neil, if slightly more impressionable. "He was sitting there..." Keith recalls, "...strumming his guitar. I think he must have been self-taught because he had the strangest playing style. After a while he played me a particular piece which he claimed he'd just composed. It sounded quite good. I was impressed. Only later did I realise he'd copied it from a Cream album".

Fantasies apart, Keith and Neil became good friends, meeting regularly during the holidays. Eileen had by this time left Bedales for a job as a nursing auxiliary in a geriatric hospital, but Bob was still caretaker at the school and so Neil and Keith had the run of the place during the holidays. They played billiards, table tennis, smoked, lay around. Back in the caravan they listened to Fleetwood Mac, Donovan, Captain Beefheart, Fairport Convention, wrote songs together, and stayed up half the night in pursuit of truth and beauty. By this time Neil had acquired a stereo system, and night after night would pass with the bass wound up and the music at pain threshold while Eileen sat over her knitting in the nearby cottage nodding over the foibles of youth and wondering whether noise could do structural damage.

By this time, according to his friends, Neil had developed a definite style. He was plausible, interesting and strong willed. Earlier than most, he'd discovered the potency of one-to-one contact, of paying people the enormous compliment of actually *listening* to them, and it was a habit that made a particular impression on women, as a schoolfriend called Jan Heidecker recalls. "The thing about Neil was that he used to pay you *all* his attention. If he was sitting in a crowded room at a party or something it wouldn't matter. Whoever came in, whatever happened, he'd ignore it. The important thing was talking to *you* and the really important thing was you talking back to him and you never realised at the time but that was very potent and quite dangerous because he was very perceptive and without even seeming to try he'd make you tell him things you'd never dream of telling anyone. He'd play games with you, but they were games he'd always win".

Keith Wilde was another frequent witness of the Slatter style. "He used to have an amazing line with the birds. We used to go out in the evenings to pubs and so on and he'd start some incredible lines of chat. His favourite gambit was reading palms. Most people find that irresistible and Neil's pitch was all the more effective because he actually believed all that stuff…. they lapped it up".

Without doubt, as he grew older, Neil found no problem acquiring girlfriends — though many of them he left with an uneasy feeling that they'd been somehow taken advantage of and then discarded. But the bruises weren't entirely of Neil's making. Among his many passions was a local girl called Gina in whom he displayed more than a passing interest. The details are far from clear, chiefly because Neil himself refuses to discuss it, but the relationship came to an abrupt end when Gina went off with a local estate agent thus acquiring — in Neil's eyes — enhanced status. He made a brief if spectacular attempt to win her back by scaling a drainpipe and breaking into his rival's flat but this ploy backfired when he found them both in bed. What happened thereafter is still a mystery, but for years to come Gina remained important to him. Not least, one suspects, because she rebuffed him.

Either way, Neil was by now nearing the end of his days at Petersfield Secondary. In his last year he was appointed Deputy Head Boy, and passed enough 'O' levels to earn a place at Sixth Form College, at nearby Havant. There he found the regime unexpectedly restrictive, and expressed his thoughts on the matter by trying to form a branch of the National Students Union. This, plus an unexplained absence abroad, earned him the disapproval of the College authorities, and his studies came to an abrupt end when they invited him to leave.

Eileen and Bob Slatter, Neil's parents

Already working evenings and weekends at the Fine Fare supermarket in Petersfield, Neil was able to convert this job to full-time employment. Officially billed as 'Trainee Manager, Frozen Foods and Delicatessen Department' Neil found the job surprisingly interesting. Skills like bacon slicing intrigued him and he was able to practise his charm on the three women to whom he was boss.

The real action, though, was reserved for weekends and it was at this point that Neil began to spread his wings. His guide and mentor, once again, was his brother Robert, by now living in a flat in South London. Robert offered an entrée to the whole early seventies world of gentle people, good vibes, and brown rice. One of Neil's first glimpses of this world was the Seasalter Pop Festival, held in a large field on the north Kent coast in the summer of 1976.

They'd driven down there, Neil and his brother, in Robert's minivan, not knowing what to expect and therefore surprised at the line of police drawn up across the country lane which led down towards the sea. The police were brisk. Neil and his brother were strip searched for cannabis and other substances, pronounced clean and permitted to enter the festival. There they found the tents and the fires and the stalls selling vegetarian food; the hordes of mongrel dogs and the flaxen-haired women in long cotton skirts with armfuls of children. Up on the stage the bands came and went, and all around them, while the music played, there were migrant families from the Welsh hills talking and laughing and sharing food, renewing friendships begun in communes way back. It was all very gentle, and very peaceful, and Neil, in particular, was much impressed. It had, he thought, a mediaeval quality, an echo of something long gone. More than that, he was with his brother again, confirming and exploring a relationship which had always been important to him. Now, freed from school, Robert represented a wider world. He travelled abroad a lot. He knew interesting people. He made it his business to get about a bit. It was all heady stuff.

Back at work amongst the frozen foods and sliced sausage at Fine Fare, Neil began to look around for another job. Part of him wanted a change — more money, different faces, a new challenge — and before long he'd landed a job with an engineering works down the A3 in Portsmouth. The job involved feeding steel billets into one end of a machine and measuring every hundredth screw that came out of the other. It was far from challenging, but it paid well and within weeks he was able to swop from normal working hours to the night shift, which meant only four shifts a week. This gave him more time for his music and his friends, and he redoubled his efforts to organise various fellow musicians into a regular band.

Neil's only problem at this point was transport. From Petersfield to Portsmouth is twelve miles and the round trip four times a week was costing him a fortune in fares. Accordingly, he'd sunk his first three week's wages into a downpayment on a motor cycle: a blue Honda 175 CD.

The job in Portsmouth lasted nearly a year. Four nights a week he rode down the A3 to his post beside the screw-making machine, and four mornings a week he rode back up to the cottage in Steep to sleep off the night's work. By now eighteen, he had money, good looks, presence. Weekends he'd spend playing his guitar, or turning out for Petersfield Rugby Colts, or simply riding around on his new bike catching up with his ever widening circle of friends. Life, in short, was OK. If he ever paused to take stock, which was highly unlikely, he would have readily admitted to a sense of contented aimlessness, of getting into anything and everything that moved, of relationships counted rather than cared about, and of a general sense of drifting wherever the vibes felt good. In Eileen's eyes, he was simply her busy adolescent son, rushing around, out most of the time, utterly normal. Bob viewed his activities from a distance and felt, on occasions, perplexed. But Neil was Neil. Then came Toni.

Toni he first met at a flat in Guildford where he made regular calls. She was married to a man with a reputation for violence and Neil remembers her sitting in a corner of the room, cross-legged, chain smoking, out of her mind on a mash of prescribed barbiturates. He liked her on sight and knew enough about her marriage to feel the first stirrings of sympathy.

Toni was 19, attractive, medium height, with a strong, open face under a mass of dark brown hair. A chaotic childhood had given her a somewhat happy-go-lucky attitude to life, and at sixteen she'd met her future husband at a holiday camp on Hayling Island. She'd been working in the snack bar. He'd been a kitchen porter. Over the next few months they saw more of each other and within a year they were married. The marriage was a disaster, quickly degenerating into what the divorce decree nisi later termed "irretrievable breakdown". According to Toni, her husband was totally unpredictable. Most of the time she spent trying to avoid the outbursts of temper that could all too swiftly lead to violence. After a while, depression gave way to fear. "It was awful. Things just kept going from bad to worse. The more dominant he became, the less easy he was to stand up to. At first I'd try to argue, but it was never any good. Either he'd sulk, or turn nasty. And if that happened, there was literally nowhere for me to run. There were lots of other people living in the house, but I think they were as frightened of him as I was. I often wondered whether he had a psychiatric problem. Either that, or perhaps I did."

Driven to semi-dependence on Largactil, a powerful tranquilliser much favoured by the Prison Service, Toni frequently thought of running away but was too frightened of the consequences. "I knew what he could do and I was terrified he'd come looking for me. He had a fantastic capacity to hate."

It was at the end of a particularly gruelling period, with Toni beginning to doubt her own sanity, that Neil arrived. "The first time I saw him I didn't really talk to him but he was impossible not to notice. He was very arrogant, very pleased with himself, but he was big, too, and very good-looking. I definitely fancied him."

Weeks later, Neil and Toni met again, this time at the flat of mutual friends in Haslemere. Beyond caring about the consequences, Toni had finally left her husband and was trying to regain a little sanity before deciding what to do next. She had neither money nor the self-confidence to risk living alone; what she wanted was protection and a little peace.

For his part, Neil was definitely interested. Toni's husband had by this time discovered Toni's whereabouts and her time at the Haslemere flat was therefore coming to an end. For Neil it was a natural instinct to offer her yet another refuge for her carrier bags and her rampant paranoia. For the time being he wasn't quite sure where, but Toni was more than grateful for the invitation. "He definitely thought he was God's gift, but I liked him. I was a complete mess and he was big enough and confident enough to take care of me. It was marvellous. He just took over. I think it must have been his upbringing. He just didn't believe that men actually hit women, that it actually happened. He was what I needed. He felt very safe to be with".

At this point, with Toni on the verge of leaving the Haslemere flat, two incidents happened, both of them significant in the light of later events. The first was a visit from her husband. Neil was already in the flat and the pair of them came face to face. Toni began to shudder at the probable consequences, but Neil simply turned away and resumed his conversation with Toni. "It was quite amazing. He just ignored him, as if he wasn't there. That really got up his nose but Neil couldn't have cared less. I saw the hatred in him, and I saw the way he was trying to will Neil to do something provocative, but Neil just soaked it all up. He was great. He'd said he'd look after me, and he was as good as his word. He was terrific".

For Toni, this incident confirmed her faith in Neil, but it also turned out to be the prelude to an ominous and disturbing event. A few days later a pack of Tarot cards arrived through the post at the Haslemere flat. The Tarot comprises a pack of 78 painted cards, originating in Italy in the fourteenth century, but long since accredited with supernatural

Toni

associations. In the eyes of many, they're not to be taken lightly —
certainly not by Neil who was deeply fascinated by the occult. For
years he'd been buying various obscure books from local junk shops —
volumes on necromancy, astrological lore, and white magic — and
more recently he'd supplemented his reading by long conversations
with local practitioners of both the black and white arts. One of them, a

self-confessed white witch, had already warned Neil that one day he'd have to face disability, but the prospect still seemed remote.

Now though, with the arrival of the Tarot cards, Neil was obliged to take a closer interest. There was no indication of where the cards had come from, but when he and three friends sat down around a table to "work" the cards, he began to pick up a spine-chilling message. The cards were handed round for a while, held, questioned and finally reshuffled. At last, when Neil began to draw them, the message was confirmed. The cards foretold impending doom and as they came out, one by one, it became clear to Neil that he was confronting a numbered sequence of five days. The cards had arrived on the sixth of July. In five days it would be the eleventh.

By this time, Toni had left the Haslemere flat and was living with friends of Neil's at Churt, a small village about four miles from Hindhead. The flat was part of a rather grand house with spacious gardens and a swimming pool, and Toni shared a handful of rooms with three others. She didn't have a bedroom to herself, but there was good music and peace and frequent visits from Neil who was still living with his parents over at Steep.

As the worst of her bruises began to subside, the relationship prospered. She knew enough about Neil to guard against a serious involvement, but he was interesting, and sure of himself, and it was easy to make allowances for his wilder stories. His sexual demands were enormous but in return he gave her back her self confidence and a certain peace of mind and for that she was extremely grateful. "In those last few weeks he made me better and I'll never forget that. He gave me back a little bit of me again..."

One consequence of Toni's convalescence, curiously enough, was the realisation that she had to make it by herself, that stepping from one relationship straight into another was simply risking a further bout of paranoia and Largactil and all the associated horrors. Not that Neil would ever beat her but he was definitely a man, and men — for the time being — were best kept at a distance. Accordingly she decided to return to London and live for a while with her mother.

"The day I actually decided to leave Neil was a beautiful sunny day. We'd got up really late, way after lunch, and we'd decided to have something to eat but there was no food in the place. So Neil said he'd ride down to the shop and pick up some bread and fruit and stuff. He met Tim, a friend of ours, in the hall and he said he'd go along too. When they'd gone I phoned my mum and told her I was coming home. Then I got all my things together and packed my two carrier bags and

11

left them by the front door, ready for when Neil came back. I was going to explain it all to him and ask him for a lift to the station. I knew he'd be upset and everything but I had to do it and it was better done now than later. OK, I'd used him, but I was sure he'd used me back. I was probably one of hundreds. It was nothing personal. In fact I liked him very much. It was just that I didn't want to get involved again, not that quickly".

Toni waited for a while for Neil and Tim to reappear. When they didn't she assumed they'd been waylaid by friends. She sat down and made herself some coffee. Then she listened to records. At five there was a ring at the door. She went to answer it, half wondering what Neil had done with his key. When she opened the door, she found herself looking at two policemen, one of them holding the remains of a blue crash helmet. He proffered it. She recognised it at once as Neil's.

"What's happened?" she said.

"There's been an accident..." the policeman said, "...I'm afraid it might be nasty".

She gazed at him a moment, then nodded. The date was the eleventh of July.

Chapter Two

Haslemere Ambulance Station lies beside the A286 on the long uphill climb out of the town towards Guildford. It's a long, low modern building in neutral brick, dominated by four large blue garage doors. On the afternoon of the eleventh of July, 1977, the afternoon shift began at three o'clock. Their first call came at four.

The two men on duty that afternoon were Jack Boxall and Frank Dominie. Boxall had fourteen years of service behind him, but Dominie — twelve years younger — was barely a month out of training school. His memories of the next hour are particularly vivid.

The call to Haslemere had come on the control frequency from Surrey Ambulance HQ at Banstead. A woman had dialled 999 from a call-box at Churt and reported an accident on the A287 just west of the village. The details were vague but she'd spoken of two men lying in the road beside a motor bike. They were both motionless.

Boxall and Dominie ran the ten yards from the rest room to the ambulance bay, Boxall taking the wheel and pulling the ambulance — call sign 'Hotel One' — out onto the main road. Switching on the two-tone horns, he pushed down through Haslemere and out into the country beyond. The direct route from Haslemere to Churt goes through Hindhead, eight miles of narrow roads, frequent bends and dawdling mid-summer traffic. Churt itself is a tiny village, and on the far side the road winds left, crests a slight hill, and then descends into a gentle right hand bend. On the left, the road is flanked by a tall stone wall which surrounds a cottage. Beside the wall, Boxall and Dominie found what they were looking for. According to their log, the time was now 16.12.

"I remember a bus..." Dominie says, "... and three or four onlookers, and all this shopping all over the road. Soap powder, and some bread, and lots of apples. The apples were everywhere. The two lads were still lying in the road, one of them by the wall, the other out across the white lines".

13

Boxall pulled the ambulance up beside the bus and the two men jumped out. Dominie went to the body in the middle of the road while Boxall attended the one by the wall. On the face of it, Dominie's patient — Tim King, the pillion passenger — had priority. "He looked by far the worse. He had a nasty wound in his left thigh and abrasions all down his left side. His shirt was ripped where he'd hit the road, and his arm and elbow were pretty bad as well". Suspecting a fractured thigh, Dominie ran back to the ambulance for a box splint, a long green corset of stiffened sponge, to bind around the leg and thus immobilise it.

Boxall, meanwhile, was with Neil. "To begin with he looked OK. There weren't any obvious injuries and his position looked quite good. He was lying on his back and there was no restriction to his airway so he had no trouble breathing. I think he'd tried to move, to get up or something, and his helmet was down there beside his head. The only thing he complained about was a numbness in his legs and feet. That made me think a bit...."

Telling Neil not to move, Boxall went across to give Dominie a hand with Tim. Dominie had by this time bound the leg wound and encased the leg in the box splint, and the two men lifted Tim onto a stretcher and eased him into the left hand side of the ambulance. Dominie nodded in Neil's direction and lifted an inquiring eyebrow but Boxall shook his head. "I don't like the look of him..." he said, "...I think it might be his spine".

Ambulancemen are trained to take special precautions with spinal injuries. Any movement at all can make an existing injury worse, and a tailor-made stretcher has been developed to cut handling to a minimum. Called a 'Scoop' or orthopaedic stretcher, it's made of thin sheet metal with a tubular aluminium surround, and divides lengthways, thus enabling ambulancemen to insert it beneath a body from either side. Adjusted for length and reconnected, it's then loaded into the ambulance in the normal way. Thus the patient can arrive at hospital with no appreciable adjustment to his position after impact, a vital consideration if a spinal injury is later confirmed.

Neil, decided Boxall, was an ideal candidate for the Scoop, and the two men divided the stretcher and eased it carefully beneath his body. Neil, fast losing touch with his lower limbs, watched the busy men with curiosity. "It was the strangest feeling. Once the pain had gone, I didn't care. I almost felt relaxed."

With the stretcher secured beneath him, Neil was carried gently into the waiting ambulance, and lowered onto the bench across the aisle from Tim. By this time Boxall was getting seriously concerned about the state of Neil's health and decided to remain in the back while Dominie took the wheel. At 16.25, thirteen minutes after arriving at Churt, the ambulance set off for the Royal Surrey County Hospital at Guildford.

By this time, Neil was flitting in and out of consciousness — lucid one minute, unconscious the next — and Boxall was aware that he was beginning to lose his grip. "In these situations it's very, very important to keep contact... the patient's best friend is himself. You've got to keep them talking. You ask them constantly about anything at all, how it happened, how they feel, where they were going, where they live. In Neil's case it was difficult. I kept asking him about the apples but he was beginning to go under and he was very befuddled. He kept repeating himself all the time, like they all do. He kept on about his mate — is he OK? — time and time again. By the time we'd got to Hindhead, he'd lost all feeling in his legs. I remember asking him if he wanted to urinate but he said he'd no idea, because he couldn't tell. By that point I was pretty sure his spine had gone".

Upfront in the driving compartment, Dominie was doing his best to flatten out the bends and bumps on the road back through Hindhead to Guildford. "I remember going ever so careful, being so new, and driving around the Punchbowl trying to cut out all the sharp corners and things, and seeing Jack there in the mirror, standing between the pair of them in the back, and then Jack opening the partition between us and telling me to get a priority".

Radio reception around Churt, even on the police and ambulance frequencies, is notoriously bad, but back on the high ground around Hindhead, Dominie was able to re-establish contact with his Controller at Banstead, and he now radioed ahead and asked for a priority clearance. This involved giving Neil's age, sex, and suspected injuries to Control who passed them on to Guildford, thus ensuring a reception committee of doctors, nurses and porters standing by at the Royal Surrey. At the very least it would mean immediate treatment; at best it might save his life.

Horns blaring and headlights on, the ambulance forked left off the start of the Guildford by-pass, and then wound down the Farnham Road into the city itself. The Royal Surrey County Hospital (since converted to a geriatric hospital) lay at the bottom of the hill on the left hand side. The access is tricky, down a steep ramp, up another, and then right and left through a warren of narrow alleys to Casualty Reception round the back. The ambulance arrived at 16.50 and Boxall

15

and Dominie carried Neil across the tarmac and into the reception area, returning immediately for Tim. By the time they were back inside with Tim, Neil was already disappearing down a corridor towards the X-Ray Department.

Back at the flat in Churt, Toni tried to absorb what had happened. The police had departed, leaving behind them two helmets, a sandal, a pendant chain and the news that Neil was en route to Guildford in the back of an ambulance. Now, with the police gone, she tried to work out what to do. First she needed transport. She ran downstairs and out into the warm afternoon sunshine. The elderly couple who owned the big house were relaxing by the swimming pool. She tried to tell them what happened, about Neil and the accident and the hospital he'd gone to in Guildford, but it came out too fast and in the wrong order, and in the end she refused their polite offer of a cup of tea and made off towards a friend's cottage nearby.

The surest route lay back along the main road, a walk of perhaps ten minutes, but her instincts told her there was a short cut through the pine woods at the back and as she plunged into the trees she desperately tried to maintain her sense of direction. Within minutes, though, she was totally lost and when she finally found the cottage she

The bend near Churt where the accident happened

16

was exhausted. Once again she poured out her story, hopelessly muddled, but she got the name of the hospital right and her friend at once offered her a lift. Alas, he didn't have a car. Would the pillion seat of his clapped-out Honda be OK? She swallowed hard and nodded. Nothing she'd learned in the last hour had softened her mistrust of motor bikes, but she had no choice. If Neil was still alive, it was her duty to be there.

The Intensive Care Unit at the Royal Surrey Hospital was on the first floor. It contained five beds with a separate cubicle containing a sixth. Beside each bed there was a small armoury of sophisticated medical equipment to keep patients alive in the twilight zone between recovery and death. The unit was staffed day and night by a specialist team of doctors and nurses under the guidance of a consultant in charge. Attached to the team was an Associate Specialist in Orthopaedic and Trauma work, and he was the first to interpret the evidence of Neil's X-Rays. A single glance at the smoky grey images gave him no room for doubt. "The X-Rays revealed a fracture dislocation between the fifth and sixth cervical. The amount of displacement was compatible with severance of the cord." In other words, Neil had broken his neck.

The human spine comprises a column of bones, twenty-four in all, called vertebrae. For the sake of classification, they're divided into three different categories. The top seven bones are called 'cervicals'. They run from the shallow ball and socket joint at the top of the spine on which the skull rests to the seventh cervical (or 'C7') between the shoulder blades. Next are the twelve thoracic vertebrae ('T1'-'T12') which support the ribs. Below these are the five big lumbar vertebrae ('L1'-'L5') then the five fused bones of the sacrum, and the spine ends in a tail-like structure known as the 'coccyx'. On average, the human male spine measures between 18 and 25 inches.

The job of the spine is twofold. On the one hand it provides the central pole in the body's scaffold of bones and on the other it offers a protected passage or canal for the spinal cord, a column of nerve fibres about the diameter of a man's finger. The spinal cord is an extension of the brain and itself acts as a kind of telephone exchange, carrying messages to and fro between the brain and all other parts of the body. The messages are of two kinds: sensations transmitted from the body's nerve ends to the brain, and commands transmitted back again to various muscles. Nerve branches leave the cord at various levels, providing a network of appreciation and command on which the brain depends for conscious control of the body's actions.

Unlike bones or muscles, the nerves of the central nervous system do not normally recover from serious injury, so severe damage to the spinal cord will cut the brain off from particular parts of the body, a condition more normally termed 'paralysis'. How much of the body is affected depends on the level of the injury: the higher the injury, the more of the body will be paralysed. Injuries above C3 (the third cervical) are almost always fatal because the respiratory muscles are paralysed and make life without an artificial respirator (the so-called 'iron lung') impossible.

With its column of bones and intermediary discs of gristle, the spine is immensely strong and surprisingly flexible. Under most circumstances it can withstand a great deal of pressure without serious damage. But there's obviously a limit, and the spine is at its most vulnerable where its curve is most pronounced. This occurs between the fourth and sixth cervicals ('C4' and 'C6'). Neil's neck was broken at exactly this point and although the spinal cord doesn't show up on X-Rays, the severity of the fracture left the doctors little room for doubt. Even if the spinal cord wasn't actually severed, then it had been sufficiently damaged to cause permanent paralysis below the level of the broken fifth vertebra.[1] For the next twenty-four hours, the doctors' job would be to try and confirm this appalling prognosis.

The first Eileen Slatter knew about her son's accident was a knock on the door of the family cottage in Steep. Just in from her job at a local geriatric hospital, she was standing by the stove in the tiny kitchen when she heard footsteps on the gravel path outside. Looking through the window, she recognised the Bedales School bursar. The police had telephoned the school and he'd come running down across the playing fields to break the news.

At first Eileen didn't believe it. She cross-questioned the man, but he could only confirm what he'd heard on the phone. Frightened, and feeling slightly sick, she phoned her second son, Robert, and told him what had happened. Neil was badly injured, possibly dead. They'd taken him to hospital in Guildford. Bob, her husband, was away on Dartmoor camping with a party of Bedales kids. She and Robert must get to Guildford at once. Robert agreed. He'd be round in minutes.

Back at the hospital, Neil was put on traction. Traction is a method of pulling the spinal column straight again by lying the patient flat on his

1 *In 95 per cent of spinal injuries, the cord isn't actually severed, but the swelling within the spinal cord is quite enough to cut off the blood supply to the nervous tissue, and thus cause the tissue to die.*

back and hanging a set of weights from his head. The weights, up to ten pounds, are suspended on a cord which runs over a pulley and is finally attached to a pair of tongs. The tongs are made of steel and look a little like the kind of headphones supplied by airlines for in-flight entertainment. Each of the two points of the tongs are bedded into the skull in specially drilled shallow holes in the temples. The system sounds crude, even mediaeval, but careful support beneath the head keeps the patient painfree, if totally immobile, and gives the spine a chance to realign itself. It also helps to control the internal bruising and bleeding which may be applying extra pressure to the injured spinal cord. To work properly, traction has to be maintained for many weeks.

Of these details, Neil hadn't the faintest idea. "At that stage I had very little awareness of the whole thing. I wanted to know what had happened, and whether there'd been an accident, but I was never able to remember what they told me. If you'd have mentioned the word traction, I wouldn't have had a clue what you were talking about."

In Neil's case traction was an obvious start to treatment, and after the minor surgery necessary to drill the tong holes in his skull, Neil was wheeled into the Intensive Care Unit. Here, the medical team completed their examination. Initial tests had already established that Neil's general condition was quite stable. At 84 his pulse was satisfactory and a blood pressure reading of 110/70 gave no cause for alarm. He had no obvious head injuries, his chest was clear, his heart was normal, and his abdomen was soft with no sign of masses, rigidity or tenderness. He had minor abrasions on the left wrist, the left thigh, and the left patella (kneecap), but his pelvis showed no signs of serious damage. The pupils in his eye were "normal and equally reactive". Only the damage to his spinal cord gave cause for real alarm. Below the level of his shoulders, he could now feel nothing.

As the daylight began to fade outside the window, the medical team began a series of tests round Neil's body. Neil was far from alert but he was conscious enough to be able to carry out commands and this he tried to do. But as the examination progressed, it began to confirm the doctor's worst fears.

In response to commands, Neil couldn't move his toes, or feet, flex his legs, hands or arms. Below his upper chest, he was unaware of heat or cold on his skin, or the prick of a needle. Paralysis of the lower half of the body, including the legs, is called paraplegia. Paralysis of all four limbs is called tetraplegia (in America, 'quadriplegia'). Both conditions require a lifetime's careful management, and the doctors were already thinking in terms of an early transfer to a specialist unit. In the

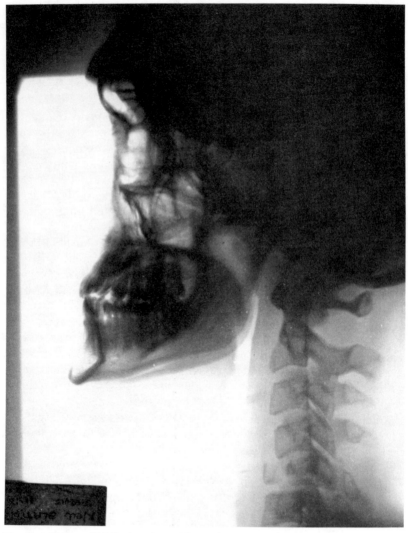

The first X-Ray of Neil after the accident. The damaged vertebra is the fifth from the top.

morning, they'd call Stoke Mandeville.

Toni arrived at the Guildford Hospital in the early evening, still shaking from the sixteen-mile lift on the back of her friend's bike. She explained who she was and asked to see Neil but at first they said it was out of the question. He was bad, very bad, and it was no time for visitors. She accepted the refusal with a nod and slumped into one of the plastic moulded chairs in the waiting room. At least he was still alive, that was something.

After a while a nurse approached and said she'd now be allowed to go up and see him. She followed the nurse upstairs and into the Intensive Care Unit. The room was quiet, except for the ticking and whirring of the various life support systems, and there she found Neil on his back with eight pounds of traction weights suspended from the tongs embedded in his skull. "He was quite conscious, just lying there. They hadn't cleaned his face at all and I remember wiping away the dirt from his eyes. We had quite a sensible conversation. He knew exactly who I was and one of the things he kept going on about was the shopping. "I got the shopping, didn't I?" he kept saying. Then he'd ask me over and over again whether he'd had an accident and how he couldn't feel anything in his legs. At one point there was a motor bike going up and down outside the window and that gave him the real screamers. He was so bad they had to go outside and stop it".

Eileen arrived with Robert an hour after Toni. At first she couldn't find Neil, though enquiries in one of the casualty cubicles revealed Tim having his leg dressed, but finally she was directed upstairs to the Intensive Care Unit. "I remember going in there and seeing all those other people, all that human wreckage from car smashes and so on, jaws wired up, that kind of thing, people on machines and thinking somehow that Neil was going to look like that as well. But, he didn't. Apart from the traction he looked perfectly normal. I couldn't believe it. I just kept saying "He will be alright, won't he?"

Toni was already at Neil's bedside and the two women met for the first time, formal introductions confined to first names and a nod of mutual sympathy, and they sat there for the next couple of hours while Neil enquired ceaselessly about the shopping and the fate of his beloved motor bike. He was also convinced he was still holding the motor cycle keys, a fixation which stayed with him for many days, and from time to time he'd plead for someone to take the keys away. The two women did their best to comfort him, exchanging glances over his head. His hands were quite empty, lying still and lifeless on the crisp white sheets.

Later in the evening, the doctor in charge of the unit called them into a side office. Toni remembers him sliding the X-Rays out of an envelope and clipping them to a viewing box on the wall. "He was very calm, very straightforward. He showed us an X-Ray of Neil's neck and he explained that the neck was broken and it was really strange

21

because I think I was expecting to see a black line or something on the X-Ray but it wasn't like that at all. He showed us where the break was, and how the bones were all out, and then said it was really serious and that Neil would probably be paralysed from the neck down. I think it was at that point that I decided to stay. Apart from anything else, he wouldn't let me go. Every time I left his bedside, he'd start screaming for me. So I phoned my mum and told her that I wouldn't be coming home after all... you know.... because of Neil. Under the circumstances, it was the least I could do".

As far as the specialist was concerned, Neil's prognosis was very poor indeed. "In my opinion, his goose was cooked from the time he hit the road. If a patient's going to recover, the signs are usually there within two or three hours of the accident. Otherwise it's probably hopeless. In Neil's case we were possibly dealing with a transacted or severed cord. It's always sensible to give a guarded prognosis as far as the patient and his relatives are concerned, but when they asked, I had to tell them he'd probably be paralysed for the rest of his life. His mother took it very calmly. I don't know whether it sank in".

After the brief conversation with the doctor, Eileen returned to the Intensive Care Unit with Toni and stayed beside Neil for another hour. She remembers staring fiercely at his hands, willing them to move again, and when he began to complain of dryness in the mouth she asked the nurses for something to drink but they gave her a bag full of ice cubes instead to moisten his lips because flat on his back, there was a danger of him choking on liquids. With his chest paralysed, one of the things he'd never be able to do properly again was to cough.

The next day was a Tuesday. On Dartmoor, Bob Slatter looked up from an early campfire breakfast of sausages and beans to see a pair of policemen labouring up the hill towards him. At first he assumed they'd come to check on the welfare of Viscount Linley, Princess Margaret's son, who was one of the party, but when the police arrived it was Bob they wanted to talk to. They broke the news about Neil and as soon as Bob had packed a bag, they gave him a lift to the station at Newton Abbott.

By mid-afternoon, several changes of train later, Bob was back at Petersfield station where his eldest son Graham was waiting to pick him up. "I remember he was very tired and very worried. The police hadn't had much to go on and he simply didn't know what had happened. I did my best to explain that Neil wasn't dead, but that the injury was pretty serious, but he didn't really twig until he saw Neil in hospital, and even then I don't think he could take it all in. He just couldn't comprehend what was happening. Not to his Neil".

Over the next three days, Eileen and Bob came and went while Toni stayed at the hospital. For reasons which she doesn't fully understand, the nursing staff in the Intensive Care Unit permitted her to stay at Neil's bedside, feeding her with soup and toast from a small auxiliary kitchen nearby and giving her a white coat to wear. Every time she tried to tip-toe away to snatch an hour's sleep or a cigarette Neil knew immediately and called out for her, over and over again, until she returned. Once, on the third day, he began to move, pulling his arm across the sheet, and she found herself grinning at him, knowing that he'd done it, that the doctors were wrong, that everything was going to be OK again. She called a doctor, told him what had happened, and he nodded and looked down at Neil as if he hadn't heard, suggesting casually that Neil's arm was in the way of something he was about to do and would he move it please? Neil did, a tiny spasm of movement, and Toni found herself laughing. She was right. Everything was going to be fine again.

By this time the Guildford team had been in touch with the Spinal Injuries Centre at Stoke Mandeville, one of nine specialist units equipped to deal with injuries like Neil's. Broken necks are mercifully rare — Guildford deals with about two a year — but nationwide there are barely 500 specialist beds and consequently there's always a waiting list. [1]

Sometimes, though, patients can be lucky, and Stoke Mandeville had responded within hours with the offer of a bed. The next day, Wednesday, the arrangement was confirmed by letter, and the transfer scheduled for Thursday 14th July.

Although he had no memory of the conversation, Neil had by now enquired exactly what was wrong with him, and the specialist had told him as much of the truth as he thought he could bear. "I explained to him what had happened, and where his neck was broken, and what it would probably mean in terms of paralysis. We knew by then he was going to Stoke Mandeville and I told him he was very lucky because it was the best unit in the land. I explained how they would keep his joints going, and prevent wasting of the muscles, and sort his bladder out, and bowels, and he took it all quite calmly. But I don't think any of it really sank in because he asked me exactly the same questions the next day".

1 *New Spinal Units at Stanmore (Middlesex) and Odstock (Salisbury) will add 20 beds and 48 beds respectively.*

By Wednesday, Toni had spent 48 hours at Neil's bedside and was totally exhausted. But try as she would, Neil refused to let her go until the nurses stepped in with a threat that the Stoke Mandeville transfer would be cancelled unless Toni be allowed to sleep. Neil appeared to give in at this point, and Toni crept out of the Unit to a bed down the corridor where she fell asleep almost immediately. Five hours later she was awake again and back beside Neil. "It was awful. He was terribly upset. He'd been crying his eyes out. He thought I'd gone."

The next day, Thursday, Neil was transferred to Stoke Mandeville. Hours before the ambulance left, Bob took Toni into Guildford and bought Toni some clothes. Toni was penniless and Bob was far from wealthy, but he was grateful for the care she'd shown his son and he wanted somehow to express it. The two of them wandered round the shops like a pair of sleepwalkers, Bob tongue-tied and confused, Toni beyond the power of decision. Finally Bob bought her an outfit in bright green and dull browns. She'd never worn anything like it in her life but she hadn't the heart to tell him. By the time they got back to the hospital, the ambulance was ready to leave.

From Guildford to Stoke Mandeville is about sixty miles. The shorter the journey time, the less risk to the patient, and the Guildford doctors had done their best to get an Army helicopter from nearby Odiham. Not only would the helicopter make the journey in a matter of minutes but the ride itself would be extremely smooth, a significant bonus. The odds were lengthening daily against Neil achieving even a partial recovery of sensation and control, but the doctors were keen to use any available means to minimise further damage to the spine. The Army, though, were obliged to send their regrets. There were no helicopters available, and so Neil had to go by road.

Transferring spinally injured patients by road is a tricky procedure. Still in traction and still in his hospital bed, Neil was wheeled out of the hospital and lifted carefully into the back of the ambulance where retaining bolts on the floor secured the bed against further movement. His body was immobilised by a corset of pillows and blankets, and an ambulanceman stayed beside him on the long journey to keep his body braced against sudden bumps or shocks. Never exceeding thirty miles an hour and keeping to the crown of the road, the ambulance crawled out of Guildford, north along the A3, and then left onto the tortuous cross-country loop around the west of London. Toni too, travelled in the back, trying to fend off a particularly nauseous attack of travel sickness. Half way, near Maidenhead, she gave up and asked the driver to stop at the next petrol station where she fled to the lavatory.

Neil watched her go, certain again that she'd never come back.

The ambulance arrived at Stoke Mandeville in the late afternoon after a journey of three hours. Stoke Mandeville is a once-small village blurred at the edges by the spread of housing estates from nearby Aylesbury, and the hospital lies on its north western edge. Like many other internationally famous UK medical centres it looks surprisingly nondescript, a collection of single story wartime huts running out at right angles from the three main axes of the hospital which jointly form three sides of an open square. The expanse of tarmac in the middle of the square is devoted to car parking, and a central avenue runs from the main road, through the entrance gates, to the main reception hall. If anything, Stoke Mandeville resembles a set of army barracks: squat, low roofed, and faintly depressing. [1]

The National Spinal Injuries Centre occupies only part of the hospital's total area and came into being in 1944 to cope with the flood of spinal cases expected from the forthcoming D-Day landings. Under the leadership of Dr. Ludwig Guttman, a central European neurosurgeon with a reputation for getting his own way, the existing hospital at Stoke Mandeville was taken over and converted. Its lack of stairs and wide corridors offered ideal access for wheelchairs, and under Guttman's vigorous guidance a whole new philosophy was evolved for the care and convalescence of patients hitherto regarded as 'incurables'. Refusing to accept that his patients should be written off for the rest of their lives and convinced that spinal surgery produced more problems than it solved, Guttman set about constructing a programme of careful nursing, physiotherapy, counselling and sheer physical effort, which transformed the expectations of men and women with severe spinal injuries. Before the war Neil Slatter would have probably been dead within three months from any number of complications. Now, on a warm summer's day in 1977, he faced the possibly grimmer prospect of a normal lifespan.

To Toni, though, viewing Neil's new home through the ambulance window, it looked like any other hospital. "Neither of us had any idea what Stoke Mandeville meant. To us it was just a very good hospital. As soon as we arrived, they took us over. They were hyper-efficient. Everything just happened around us. I was in a daze really. Off went Neil to this ward and I was just left there. It was utter routine. They obviously did it every day of their lives, and there we were, thinking

1   The new National Spinal Injuries Centre, largely funded by the Jimmy Savile Appeal, will open in 1983

25

how special Neil was, the only bloke to break his neck in the history of the world, and he was just gone, bang, like that."

Now, four years later, Neil has great difficulty remembering the first hours at Stoke Mandeville but the handful of impressions that have stuck include the feeling of endless corridors, and a constant changing of faces above his trolley, and his continuing anxieties about Toni and then the first glimpse of his ward and the sound of canned laughter from the television set at the end. Beyond that, Stoke Mandeville was a complete mystery.

The ward to which Neil was taken was Ward One X. Now it no longer exists but then it was under the charge of Sister Marion Rose, a busy, robust, forceful Welsh nursing sister with eleven years experience in the Spinal Centre. With the help of a junior sister, two staff nurses, two State Enrolled Nurses and a couple of orderlies, it was her job to see the ward's twenty-three patients through their stay at Stoke Mandeville. Few would be with her for less than four months. Most wouldn't recover any significant degree of movement. And all of them she regarded with a fiercely protective loyalty as "my boys". To her, Neil was a typical admission. Both the cause and effects of his injury were all too common and his reactions during those first few hours were exactly what she'd expect: "In those early days they're very frightened. They haven't got a clue what's going on. They're bewildered. Everything's happening around them but it's happening to someone else. It's not them at all. It's just one great catastrophic event".

Eileen and Bob, meanwhile, had made their own way to Stoke Mandeville and were told they'd be able to visit Neil as soon as the doctors had finished their preliminary tests and X-Rays. Eileen, well used to the medical world from her Petersfield job, expected few surprises from Stoke Mandeville, but here, inside the hospital, she found herself confronting the real consequences of Neil's accident. Everywhere she looked there were wheelchairs: in the car park, in the canteen, rolling up and down the corridors, parked in neat rows outside the wards. In one sense it was the logical answer to paralysis, wheels instead of legs, but for Eileen it was a profound shock. "I don't know why..." she says, "... but even after those four days at Guildford and everything they'd told us and knowing he might never walk again, I'd just never associated Neil with a wheelchair. To me, wheelchairs were for old people, the kind I looked after every day at work. Not for boys of nineteen. Not for Neil".

Killing time, Eileen and Bob went to the canteen for a cup of tea. But the tea she left undrunk on the table. After a while she walked hastily to the lavatory and began to cry.

Chapter Three

The X-Ray Department at Stoke Mandeville lies at the northern end of the long corridor which provides the main axis for the Spinal Centre. At peak times of day, after the consultants' ward rounds, it's often choked with beds, most of them carrying the tell-tale traction weights dangling from the shaven heads of recently admitted tetraplegics. For Neil and his attendant orderly, queuing for his X-Rays within hours of admission, it was just another set of ceilings, faces and voices off.

X-Rays for cervical patients are normally taken in three positions: vertically downwards onto the supine body, obliquely and from one side. With most patients the latter position is the most important and great care is taken to produce an exact image. The patient is wheeled beneath the arm of the X-Ray machine, the tube of the camera descends to neck level, and two orderlies in protective lead waistcoats pull on the patient's arms to keep his shoulders away from the stream of X-Rays. The resulting films then offer the doctors a map of the spinal injury and enable them to chart a way forward.

In most cases, the best the doctors can do is to realign the spine into a reasonable facsimile of its former self and then wait for nature to do the rest, a process which hopefully results in a fusion of the fractured vertebrae. This in no way guarantees even a partial release from paralysis. A good 'bony union' often makes no difference to the degree of handicap, while a poor repair to the bones can sometimes be accompanied by an unexpected return of sensation and control. In the area of spinal injuries there are few certainties beyond the patient's need to accept and adapt to an abrupt — and frequently permanent — change of lifestyle. But then Stoke Mandeville isn't really in the business of cure, but of adjustment: mental, physical, emotional, and lifelong.

Neil's first X-Rays showed an unstable fracture of the fifth cervical vertebra, confirming the Guildford findings. The lesion, a medical term for sudden traumatic injury, was severe enough to suggest that the spinal cord had been irreparably damaged, but Neil's consultant decided to maintain the traction and monitor progress with a further series of regular X-Rays. For Neil this would mean at least six weeks flat on his back with no possibility of movement.

At Stoke Mandeville, the major investment is in time. Patients are immobilised as long as is thought necessary for the bones of their spine to realign in the hope that some precious flicker of movement — in a hand or even a finger — may return. This may be relatively unlikely and at least one of the Centre's three consultants believes he can tell within two weeks just how final the prognosis may be, but the lack of direct surgical intervention minimises the risk of further damage. On this issue of surgery — to cut or not to cut — there are certainly other opinions. Elsewhere in England, some consultants may choose to operate on spines and stabilise the injured bones with wire or bone grafts or metal rods. This may get the patient into a wheelchair far quicker than at Stoke Mandeville and is common practice in the US where the treatment of spinal injuries is generally far more aggressive.

From the X-Ray Department Neil was wheeled back to his ward where he next submitted to a full neurological test to determine the exact extent of his injuries. A battery of checks related to a five point power scale gives the doctors a very precise indication of the effects of nerve damage, and their findings on admission serve as a benchmark for the coming months. In Neil's case these tests once again confirmed what the doctors at Guildford had suspected from the start: that all sensation and control below his upper chest had been lost. Barring miracles, Neil was a fully fledged tetraplegic, a conclusion he was far from ready to accept. "They'd say there was no response to all these tests, but in my mind it was all still happening. They'd say bend your arm or move your knee and I'd be sure I was doing it, yet when I looked, nothing happened. It's the same now. If I close my eyes, I can do anything with my hands."

Stoke Mandeville's policy towards visitors is very liberal. Unlike many hospitals, visiting hours are unlimited between 10am and 9pm, and patients' friends and relatives are encouraged to take as close an interest as possible in what goes on. The reasons for this are two-fold; firstly because it's a source of great comfort to the patients, especially those who are young and recently injured; and secondly because the medical staff know full well that the vast majority of their charges will never 'get better' in the conventional sense.

Many tetraplegics must make enormous demands for the rest of their natural lives, and it's often relatives or friends who must take on that responsibility. For Eileen Slatter, that particular penny had yet to drop, but she was grateful for the chance to be beside her son again. "I was very apprehensive, very frightened, but it helped me to be there, actually there at his bedside, and to know that he wasn't dying. Those first few days I don't think he had a clue what was going on. He was hallucinating. Talking to himself. Toni and I just used to sit there for hours, staring at his arms and legs, total concentration. We just couldn't accept he'd never be able to move them again."

For Bob too, it was very difficult to come to terms with what had happened to Neil. Never a natural conversationalist, he found it impossible to remain at his son's bedside, but prowled up and down the ward, thinking how terrible it all was, helping wherever he could, trying to turn his own sense of bewilderment and frustration into something positive and concrete. For the time being, Bedales School had given him compassionate leave from his job as caretaker but he knew he'd soon have to return and he was also worried about Toni. As she'd accepted responsibility for Neil, so he must make arrangements for her. She'd need food, support, somewhere to live. That meant money, and Bob's few savings were already stretched to the limit.

For Toni, though, life was strictly a question of getting through the next day. She'd already crossed swords with Sister Rose, who had slightly more formal ideas about dress and conduct, but it made little difference to the daily routine. "During that first week we all three used to stay at Neil's bedside all day, but in relays, taking it in turns. Eileen reacted very well. She was obviously very upset but she didn't show it very often. Sometimes we'd go down to the Jimmy Savile coffee lounge and just sit there amongst the fag ends and the empty cups, saying nothing. I think they were both so pleased I was staying around. We became really good friends. What they didn't realise was that it was so logical. With someone hurt that bad, you can't just walk away. You can't. By that stage I'd begun to suss what I was in for, how long it could all take, but I'd decided I'd stay for as long as it was necessary, for as long as I was needed, and that I'd do anything to get him better. Anything. In a way I was repaying a debt to him. He'd been very good to me, and now it was my turn."

For Neil, life was still a blur. He knew he'd swopped hospitals, he sensed people around him, voices, instructions, jokes, but the details were far from obvious. "I'd no idea of time. Seconds seemed like hours, even days. I just used to gaze up at the ceiling, inventing patterns round the cracks and telling Eileen and Toni about them. Toni used to play the game with me. She used to stare up there as well and share it all. But it used to worry Eileen out of her skull. She'd nod at everything and say yes and then rush off to tell the doctor."

Neil also suffered another obsession. It featured the motor cycle keys, still evidently clutched in his right hand. "It was strange. They were there for days and days. No one could take them out. I used to wake up with them there thinking how stupid it was to ride the bike when I was asleep, how that was really asking for trouble, how I might even have an accident and end up in hospital. So it went on, round and round, really crazy stuff."

Gradually, though, the ward began to slip into perspective. Flat on his back, unable to fit faces to voices, he listened to the conversations in the beds around him, the constant ebb and flow of chatter and small talk, until he developed a reasonable idea of the geography of the place. At this point one of the nurses gave him a pair of prismatic glasses, specially useful for spinal patients. These sit on the bridge of the nose in the normal way, but the lenses contain tiny prisms and bend the sight through an angle of ninety degrees, thus enabling supine patients to see along their bodies and out across the ward. The nurse slipped them onto Neil's nose and then stepped aside. He blinked a couple of times and then frowned. There was no doubt about it. The place was full of dwarfs. Everywhere he looked, dwarfs. Up and down the ward, past the foot of his bed, sets of heads and shoulders, dwarfs. He offered the thought to the nurse: was it a sane proposition to share a large room with twenty dwarfs? She laughed and took the glasses away. He'd been looking at the top half of fellow patients, she explained. And they were sitting in wheelchairs.

After Neil had settled into Stoke Mandeville, Eileen and Bob returned to Steep. By this time it was clear that Neil would be in Stoke Mandeville for the rest of the year and so the pair of them decided how best to reorganise their lives around the need for regular visits. Both of them were now back at work, and so weekends offered the only real chance to keep in touch with Neil but making the most of weekends meant staying up there. A single weekend visit — an afternoon at the bedside and then home again — was unthinkable, and two separate journeys — Saturday and Sunday — would cost a fortune in petrol. So Bob decided to solve the problem by towing up the family caravan and finding a nearby site. That way they could travel up on the Friday evening, spend the whole weekend at the hospital and then return for work on the Monday.

Bob duly prepared the caravan and when Friday arrived he set off for

Stoke Mandeville, but the journey came to a premature end on the A4 between Reading and Maidenhead when Bob drove into the back of another car. His own car, a Datsun 100A, was crushed between the car in front and the caravan behind, and Bob was left standing by the road in a thin drizzle wondering whether there were any limits to catastrophe. Hours later, after a complex series of telephone calls, his eldest son Graham arrived with a borrowed car and completed the tow to Stoke Mandeville where the caravan was berthed in a field near the hospital. Later that week, Bob's insurance company contacted him with the news that his car had been judged a write-off.

The caravan though, was a great help. Not only did it provide a bed for Bob and Eileen at the weekends, but it gave Toni somewhere to live until she could find a place of her own. Her money problems were eased by going on the dole. "I went down to the local office and I was very straight with them. There was a particular woman there. I explained it all to her and she was marvellous and she worked it some special way because it was obvious that the last thing I wanted was a job. So she worked it so that there was no job I was possibly qualified for or would accept and I came away with whatever it was a week plus my rent paid. At that point, of course, I was living in the caravan but I started to look for a flat at once."

Back at the hospital, Neil began to recognise the outlines of the daily ward routine. Mornings began at half past seven with a wash and brush up. Nurses and orderlies went from bed to bed with flannels and toothbrushes, a procedure which quickly lost its charms on the younger patients, like Neil. "It was always a problem because they normally came round just when I was getting off to sleep. Through the night you're turned every three hours and I never really slept properly until the early morning. But just as I was feeling drowsy, on would go the lights, and round came all these noisy people with their bowls of hot water. After that, you had no chance..."

Next came breakfast. For people like Neil, immobilised on traction, feeding was far from simple. One of the special nursing devices developed at Stoke Mandeville is the Egerton Turning Bed, a device which enables both bed and patient to lie in one of three planes, thus relieving pressure on vulnerable parts of the body. The beds are turned electrically every three hours, and the intervals are deliberately planned to leave the patient full length on his side for mealtimes, a position which makes feeding a little easier. In the early days, spinal patients are given the blandest foods while their bodies begin to work again after the trauma of the accident (foods liable to irritate the gut are especially avoided; apart from anything else, early admissions can't pass wind). In Stoke, that meant a diet of powdered foods — eggs, potatoes, etc — which Neil viewed as a grave disappointment. During the long days at Guildford and during the first days at Stoke, Neil had been eating nothing, and he'd been looking forward to something substantial but here he was swallowing mouthfuls of stuff that tasted like cotton wool. For a while, under the watchful eyes of the nurses, he persevered. But then he persuaded Toni to eat it, a transaction which she added to her mental checklist of necessary therapeutic sacrifices.

Breakfast over, the nurses next turned their attention to bladder problems. In the early weeks, patients like Neil have to have their bladders drained. Their bodies are still shocked from the accident and the bladder is unable to discharge urine. Unattended, the bladder quickly becomes distended and so three times every twenty four hours, the nurses have to insert a tiny tube called a catheter into the patient's penis and drain the bladder of urine. A careful check is kept of everything the patient drinks during the day, and this volume is matched against the outflows through the catheter. For Neil, events like this quickly became part of the new routine. "You'd think it would be very humiliating but it's strange how you just accept it. Apart from anything else, you can't feel the catheter going in or coming out, and you're totally unaware of any desire to go to the lavatory, so you simply forget all about it. Funny. I'd been going to the loo every day of my life for nineteen years, yet it all just stopped and I didn't once miss it. Absurd".

The working day on Ward One X began at nine. Mobile patients whose spine had already been stabilised, rolled away in their wheelchairs to the Centre's various departments to begin the daily schedule of physiotherapy, occupational therapy, archery, or any one of the other occupations specially designed to begin the slow return to some kind of normality. New patients like Neil also received physio-therapy at the hands of resident physios who'd arrive at his bedside with a smile and a nod and a brisk line in passive exercises.

'Passive exercise' is medical shorthand for someone doing the moving for you, and for traction patients there were two sessions of passive exercise per day. These involved the physio working her way round the patient's body, muscle by muscle, joint by joint. Toes, feet, legs, fingers, arms were all exercised through their full range of movement at least thirty times, a process which ensured that joints didn't become rigid and stiff. For Neil, it was a novel way of passing half an hour. "One of the things I remember to begin with was my left knee. The physio would bring it up vertically so I could just about see it and every time she flexed it the wound on my knee from the crash opened up. It looked horrible but of course I couldn't feel a thing. It was as if it belonged to someone else."

Hands were regarded as especially important. With a complete C5 lesion, there's virtually no movement in the fingers and so each patient had to wear a specially made splint around which the hand was bandaged. The lads in Ward One X referred to these splints as 'boxing gloves' and they had to stay on for about six weeks, after which the hand was permanently fixed in a claw-like position. Attractive or otherwise, this is of far greater use than a permanently open hand, though Neil independently decided that one claw hand and one open hand would be a neater solution. "I didn't want two claw hands so I used to bang one of them on the side of the bed. It didn't hurt of course but there was a real danger of pressure sores so they had to take the bandage off. No way did I want two claw hands, and now I'm very glad I've only got one. Claw hands give you greater strength because it uses the wrist extensor muscles to close the fingers against the palm but the open hand gives me lots of extra possibilities. I can pick up pieces of paper with it, point with it, gesture with it, express myself with it, do all those important *social* things. In the strictest terms, it's not as useful but it looks so much better. I can actually leave it around in full view without worrying what people might be thinking. It helps me stay normal..."

Another bedside interlude featured the Occupational Therapist. While the physios concentrated on keeping the body as supple as possible, the OT taught the patient how to apply the few joints and muscles at his disposal to the tricky business of coping with daily life. This later developed into a comprehensive programme, but in the early stages of traction it was fairly primitive. To Neil's amusement, his first task was to sew himself a leather wallet for his wheelchair. "They give you a piece of leather and a hole puncher and some thongs but of course there's nothing you can do so they do most of it for you. But at least it's a relationship and it keeps your mind off the ceiling for a while. My therapist was very nice. I kept suggesting she forget the leather work and teach me to turn 'Playboy' pages, but she thought it was a terrible idea".

At ten o'clock, after physio and OT, there was the daily pressure sore inspection. Of all the complications to which spinal patients are vulnerable, the most common is the onset of pressure sores. The unrelieved weight of the body on a particular area, or pressure from some other object, can quickly lead to redness and — unchecked — the beginnings of a sore. At this point the flesh decays and finally dies, the redness turning into an ugly black ulcer which will leave the body literally wide open to infection. At best, a pressure sore can mean months of careful nursing, at worst it can be fatal.

Because spinal patients have no feeling of pain below the injury, they must learn the importance of guarding against pressure sores. This means having their bodies moved at regular intervals and undergoing a daily examination for the tell-tale signs of redness. Under traction, this requires the careful attentions of a five man lifting team, and every morning in Ward One X, the team would gather round Neil, lifting him chest high, perfectly flat, while Sister Rose ran her eyes over his back and buttocks. His pillows re-positioned, his sheets straightened, and every last crumb removed, Neil would then make a gentle return to his bed, the weights still hanging from his head. The exercise reminded him of an Army manoeuvre: precise, controlled and (to those taking part) utterly unremarkable.

After the daily inspection, Neil lay back and awaited the regular ward round, a posse of consultants, heads of departments, registrars, and trainees who kept a regular check on his progress. Unlike the early Guttman days, the Spinal Centre is now led by three consultants, each of whom controls a feifdom of his own. Their regimes tend towards the autocratic, their decisions are final, and in general they see no point in holding back information from patients who want the truth. By this time, the enormity of what had happened — its cause and consequences — had begun to dawn on Neil. Through the daily barricade of bright faces, cheery greetings, and constant activity, it was impossible to ignore the fact that most of his bedmates were as helpless as he was, and that those who were up and about had simply swopped their beds for a wheelchair. Yet he still didn't ask for the truth, something which Sister Rose had long recognised as a familiar defence mechanism: "It's strange, very few patients ever ask you outright 'Will I ever walk again?' Why? Because they don't want to know, and while they don't know, there's still hope. But it does slowly begin to dawn on them. Nurses bath them, and they can't feel it. That matters. Ex-patients often say they'd have preferred to have had the truth much earlier but how can we do that? We must give them some hope. We have to take it one day at a time. We have to fill their minds with all the activity. Very few are strong enough to cope with all that bad news at once."

By design or otherwise, Eileen was a willing accomplice to this policy of discreet silence on the long term effect of Neil's injury. During those first weekends, she sat by his bed, diligently avoiding any reference to the future. "He never discussed paralysis and it was the same with me. I was determined to stay cheerful, to jolly him along. I just used to sit there with my knitting, burbling about anything that came into my head."

The main meal of the day on the Stoke Mandeville wards was lunch, and this was served at twelve-thirty. Once Neil had graduated from powdered foods, he was offered a choice of menu and developed a healthy appetite: partly because he was still young, and partly through sheer boredom. The day's offerings would be read to him and he'd indicate a preference, but lying flat on his back with no movement of his head, his initial impressions of meals were almost entirely confined to sound effects. "There'd be the rattle of the trolley at the end of the ward, and the rumble of wheels, then the clunk clunk as the side doors were opened and the clatter of lids coming off and the slurping of food from ladles into plates and then the scraping of marge onto slabs of toast."

Every meal was spoon fed to him in small, manageable bites, normally by Toni, and one consequence of regular eating was the need for regular bowel evacuations, a procedure to which every patient had to submit every two days. A laxative and a couple of suppositories were normally enough to stir the bowels into action, and the rest was accomplished with the aid of a nursing technique termed 'gentle digital manipulation'. In crude terms, that meant a nurse or an orderly putting on a polythene glove and physically helping the faeces out of the anus, yet another consequence of paralysis to which Neil would have to make a lifelong adjustment. "The real problem there was that you never knew when you'd finished. The orderlies or nurses would come round and stick these suppositories up your backside but the only real clue you'd have about the result was the smell. But even that wasn't conclusive because it could have been anyone. Sometimes there'd be four or five of us having bowel evacs behind our little bits of curtain and then the smell would come wafting down the ward and it was awful. It really was."

After lunch on Ward One X, there was another interlude with the catheter, followed by a bed turn which put Neil flat on his back again. Before him there then stretched the afternoon for reading, radio, or simply a chat with Toni who by that time had established a routine of her own. "I'd get up in the morning and take the bus down to the hospital. I'd arrive about ten. If I was the slightest bit late, Neil would always demand to know why. He was very suspicious, very possessive, very jealous. It used to wear me out. He'd want to know every detail of what I'd been doing, and where, and who with, and if I left for the last bus at night a minute early he'd start up again. I don't know what he thought I was up to or who with, but he'd go on and on about it".

Toni was allowed to stay on the ward from ten in the morning until the mid evening, and she became as familiar with the ward routine as did Neil. The long summer afternoons would be interrupted by tea at half past four, with another bed turn before the evening meal at six. After supper the nurses would tour the ward totting up each of the charges' fluid balance sheet for the day, and matching the figure against the carefully measured urine outflows through the catheters. Afterwards they circulated again with bowls of warm water and toothbrushes for the last wash of the day before a bed turn at eight, a serving of tea or cocoa, and then a couple of hours of talk or telly before the final bed turn at eleven. This last turn was scheduled to leave the entire ward flat on its back for the beginnings of sleep.

In theory, at least, the days thus rolled by, a busy framework for this strange community of mostly young men, crippled in no respect except physical, coming slowly to terms with the consequences of never again being able to walk, feel, or — in the conventional sense — make love. For most of them their paralysis was the result of a sudden and totally unexpected accident. Unprepared by a congenital condition or by the slow creeping-up of a degenerative disease, they found their biggest source of comfort in each other. "There was an amazing feeling of kinship in the ward. There was a lot of sharing, and comparing, and wondering where we'd all end up. If we were honest, we were all frightened, and we'd latch onto anything — even the briefest spasm of movement — as a sign that things might yet come right."

Back at Petersfield, meanwhile, there was good news and bad. Bob's misfortunes behind the wheel continued. One wet afternoon about three weeks after Neil's accident, he was driving the school minivan on a routine errand when he inexplicably lost control on a bend. The van skidded towards the steep turf verge, tipped onto two wheels and then turned over. Thrown out, shaken, but otherwise unhurt, Bob sat beside the wreckage in the long wet grass, his mind finally beyond deciding what to do next. After a while a passing motorist stopped to help but Bob waved away his offer of a call for an ambulance. Instead he asked for Graham, his eldest son, and when Graham finally got to the scene of the accident Bob was still there, squatting in the grass, gazing into nowhere. The police had arrived by that time and Graham explained to them about Neil's accident and the effect on Bob and the police nodded, and said they understood, and ran Bob to the hospital for a check up before taking them to their respective homes. After that it was Eileen who took the wheel for the long Friday night trips to Stoke Mandeville.

At Stoke, though, things were better. They'd now been able to re-site the caravan on land adjoining a friend's house, and so they were able to enjoy the modest luxuries of warm water and proper food after the long days at the hospital. There, they'd been able to spot slight improvements in Neil, though a first visit to Neil's bedside had come as a shock to his eldest brother, Graham. "We'd never been at all close until that point but there was suddenly a change in both of us, me as well as him. Just after the accident he had a really rough time, sorting himself out, and I think that changed him. I think he grew up, very abruptly. He became very interesting to talk to. He had time, suddenly. There was no more rushing about. In those early weeks, though, he wasn't at all in command. He was very much at the mercy of what was happening around him. He used to get terribly depressed. He used to have dreams. He used to see snow outside the window. Often he'd see himself rising from the bed. Sometimes he used to imagine what the ward looked like from the outside, purely because he couldn't get out there to see for himself".

Depression is a difficult thing to remember. Mercifully, our memories rub the edges off the blacker days and if we remember anything at all, it's a feeling, a mood, rather than a set of specific events. Neil, though, has now developed an almost scientific precision about the subject. "The first depressions are during traction. You get very frustrated. As the weeks go by they start to move you up the ward and you get a change of ceiling for a while — a new set of cracks — but you can never actually do anything and that's awful. You can hear voices either side of you but you haven't got a clue what they look like. Things happen at home, like Bob's accidents, and you think it's probably your fault, yet there's absolutely nothing you can do, there's all the money they're spending on your behalf, all the petrol and stuff just getting up to see you every weekend. You know they can't afford it, and that makes things even worse. Even the visits themselves can be a problem. I was lucky with Toni and Eileen. They always arrived when they said they would. But there were others on the ward who really looked forward to the weekends and then Saturday would come and no one would arrive and then the phone would ring and every one would go quiet. Then a sister or one of the nurses would take the phone and the poor fella would get the bad news. It might be trouble in the family, or illness, or some kind of accident, or that dreaded message that the wife or girlfriend simply couldn't take any more and wouldn't be coming. That's the one that really hits you in the pit of the stomach. It's just like prison. You've got no control — and worse than that, you can't even get rid of your frustrations because of the bloody traction. You're trapped."

There were, however, the red letter days, moments of genuine triumph, milestones along the road to getting better, or at least learning to understand and accept what had so irretrievably happened. The first of these was getting rid of the catheter.

With most cervical injuries, the bladder remains non-functional for about a month. But as long as the spinal cord is intact below the level of the injury, then the body's autonomic nervous system (different to the central nervous system, and not dependent on an intact spinal cord) re-establishes control over the bladder, and the bladder begins to function again — not in the sense of the patient being able to time and control the discharge, but in the sense of simply working. The first the patient knows of this major advance is either by smell, or by someone noticing the spreading patch of damp on the sheets between the legs. In the increasingly remote world of able bodied people outside the hospital, this is called incontinence and is a source of considerable embarrassment, but in the spinal wards at Stoke Mandeville, it's regarded as a triumph.

After the urine begins to pass again, the catheterisation is cut down to twice a day, and then once, until male patients go onto a condom, a tube and a bottle. This system is simplicity itself. The patient has a condom secured to his penis with one of a number of special glues. The condom connects with a tube, which in turn leads to an expandable rubber bag which is strapped to one thigh. This is called a 'kipper'. Thus equipped, incontinence ceases to be a problem. The 'kipper' simply fills up and once full, is emptied. The system requires a little care but after the passive indignities of the catheter, it's a big step forward.

Women, of course, cannot use this system and incontinence remains an appalling handicap for women tetraplegics and paraplegics. Some have a catheter permanently inserted in the bladder, but suffer the constant risk of infection; others try and achieve some degree of control over their bladders, a process which can mean literally hours on the lavatory (hence the wry gibe 'chained to the loo'); yet others submit to an operation called an 'Ileal Diversion' in which surgeons seal off the bladder and fashion a new channel from a segment of the small bowel (or *'ilium'*) which is often then connected to a plastic collecting bag via a hole (or *'stoma'*) in the wall of the abdomen. This operation, which is irreversible, certainly frees the woman from the constant embarrassments of incontinence, but can lead to long-term kidney damage.

By now, Neil had been at Stoke Mandeville for a month. Toni continued to commute daily to the hospital on the bus, while weekends attracted a growing number of visitors. One of them was his old Steep drinking partner and fellow musician, Keith Wilde. "I remember hitching up to Aylesbury and walking into the ward, frightened of what I might find. Somehow I'd thought he'd look terrible. But when I finally saw him I was amazed. Apart from the weights and the shaven bits of his head he looked quite normal. I thought for one hideous moment he'd been conning us all."

For Neil, too, life was beginning to get back to normal. Surrounded by fellow cripples and far too alert not to ponder the next sequence of events, he began to take a lively interest in the medical details of his own progress. This is something the doctors and nurses try and encourage, and Sister Rose answered Neil's every question. "The boys are desperately interested in their charts and X-Rays and so forth and we tell them as much as possible. It helps them to help us. In this sense, spinal nursing is quite unlike any other kind. We teach them as much as possible about their bodies. They get to know the names of all the muscles but then they have very good reason to. The more they know, the quicker they'll be able to recognise the complications."

After the discarding of the catheter, the next red letter day was the removal of traction. Throughout the period of traction, doctors monitor the progress of the mending vertebrae by means of regular X-Rays and once the bones have come together and re-aligned themselves the traction is withdrawn. This is done over a period of twenty four hours, one weight at a time, until there are no weights left. That, at least, is the theory. Neil's experience was rather different. "In my case it didn't work too well. My traction tongs had been seated on the top of my skull, rather than above my ears, and this system had a reputation for occasionally falling out. As it happened, I was due to come off traction anyway, but all I remember was lying there one morning and suddenly feeling as if I'd been fired down the bed. There was a terrible scream and it took me several seconds to realise it was me. The tongs had fallen out and all the weights were on the floor. Being without the weights that suddenly was the strangest feeling. It was as if I'd suddenly opened the throttle on the most powerful motor bike ever invented. It was the ultimate take off."

Weightless for the first time in six weeks, Neil was wheeled down to X-Ray for a set of precautionary films. Once they'd been developed, he returned to the ward and waited on tenterhooks for the consultant's decision on whether or not the traction should be reapplied. The consultant studied the films for a moment, then decided against further traction and passed on to the next bed. Much relieved, Neil closed his eyes and succumbed to his first shampoo for a month and a half. "It was quite incredible. They rub in Savlon during traction to take away the itchiness, but this was the full works: warm water, bubbles, fingers on your scalp, fantastic smell. I'm not kidding. It was almost orgasmic..."

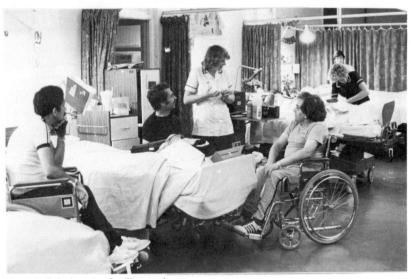

A typical Stoke Mandeville ward

Chapter Four

Sex for the disabled sounds an unlikely proposition but for Neil it had lost none of its former importance. In the first few weeks after the accident he'd had other things on his mind, but as it gradually dawned on him that pleasure stopped at the level of his shoulders, he'd begun to think about sex again. Sex had always been a source of delicious experiences, but it was also a way of saying things, of creating a special kind of dialogue, of exploring his own appetite for power and control. In a more straightforward sense, he'd also been extremely randy. He liked women. He enjoyed their bodies. He welcomed reciprocation. And try as he might, he suspected he hadn't changed. His only problem was mechanical. The end was still all-important. Only the means had gone.

Toni's constant presence at the bedside was a living invitation to reassert himself sexually, and this he did. His able bodied sex life with Toni had been brief but spectacular. He'd had a large appetite and a comprehensive repertoire, as Toni had discovered. "He'd been wildly oversexed before the accident, ludicrously so, and he wanted to get back into it again as soon as possible, just to prove something to himself, his manhood I suppose. Of course he had a bit of a problem there, especially on traction, but he'd try and get round it as best we could by the side of the bed. That was difficult for me because I ended up playing both roles: the demure little girlfriend and the grateful sex kitten. The whole thing was bizarre and I certainly wasn't that uninhibited but I'd made a conscious decision that while he was ill like this, anything went, anything that might make him feel better."

For Neil, even this was a start, the beginnings of a genuine re-entry into the kind of life that would at least resemble his able-bodied days. "The doctor used to tell me that I could manage an unconscious, reflex erection but not much else but whatever they said I used to reassure Toni that I'd still be able to have sex... partly, I think, because having children had suddenly become so important. I really did want children."

Fertility in spinally injured men is a problem. The sperms themselves are often affected by changes in the body's heat regulatory mechanisms and most men with severe spinal injuries cannot ejaculate. Various methods have been developed to overcome this handicap, including the use of a powerful vibrator, attached to the top of the penis. Another method involves the use of electrodes placed in the rectum. These stimulate certain nerve pathways and can trigger the emission of semen without the need for an erection. The semen thus obtained is stored in refrigerators and later introduced to the partner of choice.

Sex apart, Neil was rapidly approaching the next major step forward, the transfer from bed to a wheelchair. In the first place this involved a change of beds. Gone were the days of having his body turned mechanically every three hours on the Egerton bed. Instead, he was moved into another bed which divided crossways at two points. With this device, the medical staff could gradually raise the upper third of the bed and lower the bottom third until Neil's body had fully understood what it was to be semi-vertical again. This slow reintroduction to the laws of gravity would take several weeks, but would spare Neil the uncomfortable traumas of an abrupt return to the sitting position. By the end of October, he'd be in a wheelchair.

By this time, though, Neil had become an integral part of the ward. Freed from the straight jacket of traction, he'd been able to look around him, fit faces to familiar voices, and generally check reality against six weeks of detailed speculation. His findings took him by surprise. "Some of the things were obvious. It was nice to see that nurses had legs and backsides and so forth. But the strangest things were the faces on either side of me. During traction, when the beds were on one side, I'd often had a good look at the bloke next to me but we were always on our backs, lying flat, and I was amazed how different faces look when you're upright. They could have been different people."

Neil's mates were a mixed bunch. In general, most spinal patients acquire their paralysis through sudden injury, rather than the slow onset of disease. In this sense, cruelly, paralysis tends to go hand in hand with a taste for physical adventure, an equation which means that the majority of patients are young and male with no previous experience of long periods of hospital and little taste for a sedentary life. The most common cause for spinal injury is motor cycle accidents and at least one sister at Stoke Mandeville believes that the compulsory wearing of helmets has meant an increase in the number of spinally injured riders. "When they didn't wear helmets..." she says, "...they simply died from their head injuries. Now they survive, after a fashion..." Other common causes of spinal injuries are car accidents, diving accidents, domestic falls, injuries at work, and sporting accidents, especially rugby and horse riding. Of the six spinal wards at Stoke Mandeville, only one was devoted completely to women.

In terms of cause and effect, Ward One X was typical of the world of spinal injuries. Across the ward from Neil was a darkly good looking South American playboy called Alfonso. Sister Rose, ever wary, regarded him as "mad as a meat axe" but Neil had warmed to him from the start. Already an old hand on One X, he'd talked Neil through the early days of traction, sharing his experience, offering advice, and keeping an eye on Neil during the long nights. Like Neil, Alfonso had a C5 break, the consequence of a much-publicised dive from the end of Bournemouth pier, but his family were thousands of miles away and he had few visitors.

Another member of the Ward One X inner circle was Alan Jones, a nineteen year old musician whose university career had come to an abrupt halt after a particularly nasty car crash in the New Forest. Three of his fellow passengers had been killed outright, but Alan had survived with a C5 break and the certain prospect of the rest of his life in a wheelchair. Pale looking, thin and sickly, he had great charm and a lively sense of humour.

A late addition to the ward was another road accident victim who quickly acquired the nickname 'Mad Micky'. He was a paraplegic and had also suffered head injuries which gave him an irrepressible taste for repetition. Throughout the night he'd call out the same word "Nurse! Nurse!" but purely as a verbal reflex and not because he was in need of attention. For his fellow patients this was an interesting variation on the normal theme of paralysis, incontinence, and long weeks of traction, and they quickly discovered that Mad Micky would repeat any word you cared to feed him. They began with innocuous suggestions like 'cabbage' (which Micky hated) but the game quickly acquired an altogether more sophisticated dimension, much to Sister Rose's disgust.

In the bed next to Neil was a young computer programmer called John Swallow, who'd celebrated his twenty-first birthday with a mid-summer party at his parents' house. The party had ended with drunken horseplay around the swimming pool, and John's friends had brought the evening to a climax by throwing him into the wrong end.

The result was a C5 fracture, and a swift transfer to Stoke Mandeville. Depressed by his injury, anxious about his future and convinced that his girlfriend was about to leave him, John lived in a state of almost permanent depression.

On the other side of Neil was another fellow patient called Sean. Sean had been a labourer on a motorway construction site before a car accident had taken him to Stoke Mandeville, and now his tetraplegia was enlivened by frequent spasms. Spasms are totally random movements caused by new reflexes which have been set up in the spinal cord below the level of the injury. Sean's spasms were confined to his leg and on doctors' orders Sean did his best to try and control them. Sitting between Sean and Neil, Toni was able to watch his progress. "Neil was really upset by all this because he couldn't feel his legs at all. He used to check with me whether Sean had had any spasms lately and if he had then Neil would dismiss it. "He'll never control them..." he used to say. ...but Sean did. Neil was on the revolving bed at this point and every now and then he'd be back on his side with a grandstand view of Sean getting a bit of movement back, and that really upset him."

With this, Neil agrees, though he adds a postscript of his own. "It was certainly frustrating to watch other people start to move a little, but all the time I was building myself a tiny little repertoire of movements like the ability to be able to lift my arm, without much control, and slide it across my belly. That was a major advance. Then sometimes I'd gain a little bit of movement overnight, or over a few days and then I'd keep quiet about it, not tell Toni, until I'd really perfected that particular movement. One of them was raising my hands over my head. I worked on that until it was OK then I sprung it on her, like a surprise present."

As Neil began to explore what potential he had left, Eileen Slatter was also coming to terms with what had happened. "Once you got used to life on the ward, the whole thing wasn't as bad as you'd think because everyone else there was in the same situation — and in one sense Neil was very lucky. Unlike some of the other fellows, he had no other serious injuries. He had no burns, no bruises, no breaks. His body was complete. It just wouldn't work any more."

Already planning for Neil's eventual return home, Eileen was also developing her own ideas about the limits of her son's recovery. Part of the evidence she saw every weekend at Neil's bedside, but conversation with other parents gave her fresh hope, and even the hospital corridors offered the odd surprise. "They had the Paraplegic

Olympics there that summer, and that was a great help. I'd no idea just how much was possible. I remember one day seeing a man in a wheelchair coming down towards me. He was quite old, much older than Neil, and he was wheeling this chair really fast, and there were some steps, six I think, and I was horrified at what was going to happen, but at the last moment he just lifted the front wheels and bumped down the steps on the back ones, just like that, an old man. I thought he was marvellous. I think it was then that I realised that there could be a life after all".

Days at Neil's bedside, though were often far from cheerful. Prior to his accident, Neil's life had been sending him into a wider and wider orbit round the family home. He'd had a job, friends, wheels. When the time was right he'd doubtless have moved away, found a place of his own, broken the links with Steep. But that kind of decision was now beyond him, and what was left was no compensation for the end of adolescence and the beginnings of a life of his own. The result was a very real bitterness, and the target was often Eileen. "At times he was impossible. He'd really give us stick, Toni and I. We were his punching bag. We'd drive all the way up there, we'd have brought presents for him, we'd be really looking forward to seeing him and then as soon as we'd arrived, he'd start having a go; why are you so late? Where have you been? I'm sure it was pure frustration but I used to go out and sit on the loo and cry about it. It would never happen that way with the men — with Robert or his dad. They'd just sit there and he'd be laughing and joking with them, but with us it was dig, dig, dig. Sometimes he'd sort of apologise but not really. And it still happens now. He has to have a go. He can't resist it. It's part mischief, part frustration. He's always been a dominating character, right there in the thick of things, but now he hasn't got the physical means to do that, he has to try all the harder."

Toni too, remembers the grimmer side of Ward One X. "He used to offload all the time, all his frustrations, on me a bit but especially on Eileen. It didn't matter to me. I used to say to him, "As long as you're ill I don't care, you can do what you like and say what you like, it makes no difference..." But Eileen used to take it very personally. She never understood why he was so awful to her. It was just that he couldn't dominate physically any more so his tongue took over. He'd be really cruel to her. He still had to be boss."

For the medical staff on the ward, Neil's behaviour was utterly routine. Over the years they'd become used to relationships or marriages beginning to buckle under the strain of acute spinal injury.

45

Bitter, frustrated, hopelessly aware of their own impotence, husbands or boyfriends would frequently put their most precious relationships to the test of abuse and ingratitude. As a consequence, certain marriages broke down. Visits became rarer and rarer until there was only the long, final letter of self-justification, the ultimate 'Dear John' with its tangle of guilt, and excuses, and the implicit promise of committal to some kind of institution. Oddly enough, husbands have a better record of staying with disabled wives than vice versa, but in many cases the relationship is often already under pressure and paralysis simply hastens the inevitable break. Other patients, though, have the reverse experience. Bizarre as it may sound, tetraplegia can cement a good relationship and open both sets of eyes to insights and a sense of inner peace hitherto unsuspected. In some cases, this discovery can take an explicitly religious shape; in others, it simply fosters a deep sense of mutual care and devotion.

Looking back, Neil can now put his own outbursts into perspective. "I used to get physically very frustrated. I had lots of energy but nowhere for it to go except on the folks and Toni. I know I used to get very bad tempered but that's all I had. That's how bad it got. I know it was unreasonable and cruel and unfair but it was the best I could do. I'm sometimes amazed they ever bothered to come back."

Imprisoned inside a body which would no longer work, Neil often drew on his knowledge of the occult. What he needed was an alternative way of transporting his remaining senses — especially his eyes and ears — without the now impossible chore of physical movement. His mind refused to conclude an even temporary pact with his body and thus close itself off from the wider world outside the ward windows. He remained insatiably curious about his surroundings. He wanted to know what the hospital looked like from the outside, whether Aylesbury was worth a visit, how things were shaping down at Steep, and in lieu of a personal visit, he'd spend hours with his eyes closed and his few remaining muscles at rest while his mind did the necessary travelling. The technical term for this exercise is transcendental meditation, a branch of the occult regarded by many as wishful thinking, but for Neil it worked. Not only that, but it returned him to a world in which he could have some kind of confidence. "It was marvellous. I was able to abandon my body entirely. I'd simply leave it behind. I'd go back home a lot. That was my favourite trip. When Eileen came at weekends, I used to tell her where she'd been moving the furniture. Most of the time I was right and that really freaked her, but it was very important to me. With every loss there's a gain".

46

By this time, the middle of October, Neil had been at Stoke Mandeville for three months and the doctors were now certain that nothing would be lost by proceeding to the next stage of convalescence. From now on Neil would know exactly what personal physical resources were at his disposal and between them, he and the hospital had to fashion as independent a life as possible from the handful of remaining muscles.

In his new dividing bed, Neil had already been getting used to the feeling of sitting up. Every day the nurses angled his torso a little further upright, and dropped his legs a little further down, until his body was arranged in a sitting position. This is standard practice at Stoke Mandeville, and provides an important safeguard against the effects of an abrupt transfer to a wheelchair. Without this gradual adaptation, many spinal patients find it hard to cope with the novel effects of gravity. After twelve weeks of gazing at the ceiling, the blood rushes to their ankles, the ward slips out of focus and the world suddenly seems a very impermanent place. To old hands like Sister Rose, it's an all too familiar disappointment. "It's difficult. You tell them things and they often seem to take it in, yet they don't. And they always expect too much. They seem to think that once they're in that chair, everything's going to be OK. But they end up sitting in a chair for the first time in three months and they expect to be able to feel things because that's what they remember about sitting, but of course, there's nothing. It feels like they're sitting on their shoulders."

Neil though, was more cautious than most. "I expected a lot from the wheelchair, but I'd also been looking very hard at everyone else. That's one of the things you do if you lie in bed for a long time. You look at people's movements, the way they move their hands and arms, their mannerisms, the way they rub their noses, and you begin to interpret their characters from the way they use their bodies. I suppose that's one of the things Stoke offers: the time to stop and think and look around you. So because I'd been looking so hard at other people getting into their wheelchairs, I knew it wasn't going to be easy."

At this period in their convalescence, all cervical patients wear a special collar manufactured from a foam polyurethane substance called Plastazote. These are made up to individual specifications in the Occupational Therapy Department and keep the patient's head reasonably stable while his neck muscles strengthen and he learns to cope with the novel world of balance and movement.

With his collar in place around his neck, and the wheelchair drawn up beside the bed, Neil submitted to the attentions of the two orderlies who lifted him carefully out of the bed. To watching eyes, his body resembled an old sack: pyjama clad, blanket draped, and capped by an expression of acute apprehension. "It was the strangest feeling, the realisation of first sitting in a chair. It's very detached. You go through a kind of mental checklist, ticking off the bits of body that don't appear to be there. You can't feel the bum you're sitting on. You can't feel the back of the chair you're leaning against. You've no idea where your legs are or your feet except with the evidence of your eyes. It's literally like being a jelly, a big lump of jelly, sitting on a cart, going down a cobbled road. There's absolutely no control at all. You're strapped in round the chest, and your feet are on pillows to protect them from pressure sores, and there you are, after all that time, sitting, and then pretty soon, within minutes, it starts to get very black, and there's a whistling in your ears and you start losing touch and you hear yourself pleading to go back to bed. You're just confused. Pure panic. Almost like the accident in reverse."

At this stage, Toni appeared. "There he was, wedged into the chair, like a board of wood. I remember his eyes coming round to me. "That's it" he said, "I'm here. That's it". He obviously thought it would be some kind of instant cure. He couldn't understand why he couldn't do it all at once. All he wanted to do was to get back to bed."

Over the next week, Neil slowly made his peace with the wheelchair. Even with the support of the cervical collar, his neck and shoulders constantly ached with the unaccustomed weight of his head, but each day his time out of bed doubled — first five minutes, then ten, then twenty — until the end of the week when he was up for a couple of hours and permitted to explore the rest of the hospital. "The really big thing was getting outside. If you could persuade someone to push you out through the french windows, it was marvellous. The last time I'd seen the world it had been high summer. Now it was autumn. There were leaves everywhere, and big skies, and clouds, and all that fresh air. It was a fantastic feeling."

Quickly returning to the routines of a normal able-bodied day, Neil was now obliged to attend regular physiotherapy and OT classes. The distinction between the two is important. The physiotherapist's job is to work on the few muscles left at the patient's command and to ensure that they remain in good condition while the Occupational Therapist teaches the patient what can be done with these muscles. The latter is largely determined by the level of the patient's break, and the OT Department work against an informal checklist. C5s for instance, are expected to be able to wash themselves, feed themselves, shave (with an electric razor), clean their teeth, and — given the necessary equipment — type a letter; while C6s can also transfer themselves from bed to a wheelchair, dress at least the top half of their body, and — very important — drive a specially adapted car. In the grim lottery of spinal injuries, the width of a single vertebrae can therefore make a world of difference.

For Neil, as a C5 break, the list of available muscles was pitifully short. At his conscious command he had a sum total of three muscles: his deltoids, his biceps and his wrist extensors. These offered full movement in the shoulders, partial movement in the arms and a single extension movement in the wrist, and his regular physio sessions were designed to ensure that these movements became as fluid and effective as possible. Once a day, therefore, he wheeled the quarter of a mile from Ward One X to the physio department where he did a regular circuit in the specially equipped gymnasium.

One of the earliest lessons was in the now-tricky business of balance. Robbed of the muscles which enabled him to stay upright without conscious effort, Neil was sat in front of a tall mirror with a physio behind him, a precautionary hand on each shoulder. When the hands were taken away, his body began to sway from side to side and only by concentrating very hard on the image in the mirror could he prevent his body from collapsing, sack-like, to one side. Henceforth, his balance would have to be controlled visually, by constant reference to horizontal surfaces about him, and not by trusting to muscles which no longer worked.

Another exercise introduced Neil to mat work. Eight or nine cervical patients would be carefully laid flat on mats on the floor, their legs crossed, and the physios would then teach them to roll over by rocking their shoulders and using the weight of their upper bodies to tip them over onto their faces. This could later be of enormous benefit in bed, but at first the lessons were far from successful, though Neil's class quickly learned a short cut of their own. In the general flailing of arms and shoulders, they'd steal a little covert leverage from the body next door, a trick which made rolling over much simpler. The physios frowned on this practice but it was nice to be able to cheat again.

A third routine, brief at first but more concentrated later, involved strapping weights to each arm and then performing a series of exercises. This restored power to Neil's wasting muscles and enabled him to apply his new found strength to the all-important business of shifting his weight in the wheelchair. The latter meant hooking one elbow around the back of the chair and then levering his bodyweight into a different position to help prevent pressure sores. This and other techniques, he was told, would have to become second nature. Every ten minutes, for the rest of his conscious life, he must ease fourteen stone of deadweight forwards and backwards, left or right, an inch at a time, on the chair. He absorbed the news as stoically as possible. After three months on Ward One X, this at least had the scent of real independence.

The physio gym also offered a series of other exercises — with pulley bars, tilt tables and standing frames. The latter appliances are designed to give patients the gentlest introduction to the half forgotten perils of being vertical again. The tilt table resembled a stretcher trolley. Secured by straps across his knees, hips and chest, Neil was tilted slowly vertical until he was once again viewing the world from his full six feet. After a number of sessions on the tilt table, he was then transferred to the standing frame, his body secured upright by more straps, while his eyes tried to relate the surrounding perspectives to a brain more used to life in a sitting position.

In addition to the gym, Neil was also sent to archery classes. Archery is an ideal therapy for tetraplegics and paraplegics. It's one of the sports in which the disabled can compete on level terms with other able-bodied athletes, and it offers the incentive of real competition as well as effective exercise for the arms and shoulders. Stoke Mandeville boasts a specially designed archery range and Neil took to the sport with enthusiasm.

Another novelty was the sudden ability to eat without a helping hand from the nurses. The work in the physio gym gave Neil a powerful appetite, and meals became suddenly important. "Eating upright was a real treat. For one thing there was less indigestion and for another you could actually see the food — though that wasn't always a good thing. At that time I hadn't quite got the strength to properly control the fork and spoon, so they gave me straps round the palm of the hand and you tucked the cutlery into special slots to stop the food slopping around too much. It used to take half an hour to eat the simplest of meals and after a while they'd give you a knife as well to cut your own food up. That was very hard at first, but I always insisted on doing it myself because if I couldn't manage it then I simply went hungry. And going hungry is the best incentive to learning how to use a knife."

Now in his wheelchair all day, Neil's other regular visit was to the hospital's Occupational Therapy Department, a newish complex of rooms a couple of minutes wheel away from Ward One X. Here a team of eight occupational therapists and four helpers designed programmes to add as many daily tasks as possible to the patient's repertoire. The complex included a fully equipped kitchen, a woodwork room, and typing facilities, and it was in this setting that Neil and his colleagues came face to face with the practical shape that the rest of their lives had to take. With their bodies now as functional as the best medical care could achieve, there was no longer any point in avoiding the difficult adjustment to the small print of daily living. With most of their flesh unable to distinguish between hot or cold, or to recognise sudden pain, they had to learn anew the perils of boiling water, badly wired electrical equipment, unlagged hot water pipes, and the careless use of sharp knives. In Neil's case he'd already had a foretaste of disasters to come when a nursing auxiliary had left a hairdryer on his chest for the few seconds it took her to unplug the appliance. Still hot, the dryer had burned his flesh but with the nerves now dead, Neil didn't feel a thing, only afterwards when the redness on his chest turned to a blister, did Neil realise that anything was wrong. He spoke to a passing nurse and was immediately treated for the burn, but it was at this point that he realised how vulnerable he'd become. The fact that his very survival was now a strictly intellectual exercise, conducted without the assistance of the normal sensory alarms, was far from pleasant. "That was strange. You can't avoid certain conclusions and for a while I used to go round feeling very hard done by. I'd get to meet lots of paras (paraplegics) who at least had the use of their bodies above the waist — their hands especially — and I'd keep thinking why them and not me? That's crazy isn't it? Getting to a point where paraplegia actually sounds attractive."

Physio and OT schedules apart, life in the wheelchair also had its lighter sides. For the first three weeks of mobility, spinal patients are given anticoagulants (Warfarin and Didevan) as a precaution against blood clots forming in the lungs and lower limbs, and these drugs preclude drinking alcohol, but after their withdrawal there's no medical reason why life at Stoke Mandeville shouldn't include the odd visit to the local pub. This is encouraged by the hospital staff, partly because of the fresh air, and partly because it's a timely reminder of problems to come. Stoke Mandeville is a world of its own, and it's all too easy to become institutionalised. The Spinal Centre is purpose-designed for wheelchairs, and after months of care there's often an implicit assumption that the world outside the hospital gates is just as accommodating. The realisation that it isn't can be brutal, and the sooner patients start to find out about narrow doorways, awkward corners, and able-bodied lavatories, the better. As well, of course, there's the question of other people's reactions. For everyone inside Stoke Mandeville, wheelchairs are the norm; in the world outside, they can still be associated with insanity.

Cervical patients normally stay at Stoke Mandeville for four or five months before discharge, and of all the hurdles they have to cross the most difficult can be the last. Weeks before they're due to leave, patients are tactfully quizzed about their ideal choice of destination. For those who are still married, or who have some other relationship strong enough to survive the coming years of non-stop care, the decision is relatively straightforward. But for others it's far from simple. Many of the younger patients have the option of returning to their parents but feel uneasy about the consequences on both sides. For them the obligatory answer is often a transfer to a Young Disabled Unit. These offer specialist residential care and a modest degree of independence but still deny many of those everyday choices which make life worth living.

Another option is a place in a Cheshire Home. These are run by an independent charity and there are sixty-seven of them nationwide. Weekly fees are normally met by local authorities and the standard of care is very high, but for some patients they represent merely an extension of Stoke Mandeville, a high class ghetto for the keeping-together and setting-apart of fellow disabled. For these patients, the whole concept of institutional care is anathema. The physical penalties of disability are bad enough. To be mentally catalogued, boxed up, and set carefully aside, is completely unacceptable.

For Neil, in the first place, there was no choice. From the moment Eileen set eyes on him in the Guildford Intensive Care Unit, there was no question what her job was. "I knew in the end he'd be coming home. It never once crossed my mind that there could be any other way. He was my Neil and he was coming home."

Three months later, she was a far wiser woman. She'd seen enough of life at Stoke Mandeville to know what Neil's return would mean, and how profoundly her own life would change, but she was still resolved to try. She knew that between them, she, Bob and Toni must become nurse, physio, occupational therapist, cook, housekeeper, companion, confidante, and — in Toni's case — lover. Neil would need looking after twenty four hours a day, seven days a week, for the rest of his natural life. During the night, his body must be moved every three hours, during the day, every ten minutes. His bladder must be taken care of, his 'kipper' regularly checked, his bowels emptied. He must avoid a long list of inadvisable foods, and anything in excess. He must be kept away from hot fluids, exposed pipes, and every conceivable source of domestic danger. He must be moved around, read to, talked with, checked for pressure sores. Television or hi-fi controls must be adjusted for him, magazine or book pages turned over. Above all he must be convinced that life — any life — is worth living, and that the enormous change in the family's fortunes is ultimately for the best. And all this in a tiny country cottage with a single downstairs living room. The space problem Bob was already trying to ease with a modest ground floor extension, but the prospects for all of them were daunting. Quite apart from the added work-load of Neil's return, both Bob and Eileen had full time jobs they simply couldn't afford to give up.

From Toni's point of view, the future was especially uncertain. When Eileen had talked to Neil about the now-imminent return to Steep, Neil simply nodded in agreement. But Toni knew Neil far too well by now to mistake this for anything but passive compliance. "Neil wanted to get out of hospital but he didn't want to go home. He wanted his own place. While you're in hospital — cossetted and looked after and all the rest — you simply assume that all that will happen when you leave, just carry on, but of course it doesn't, unless you go into a home, and he wasn't doing that. So it was Steep or nothing, and he had to come to terms with it. From my point of view I felt a bit of an orphan. I didn't belong there, I didn't want to go there, but because Neil had no choice, then I had no choice either".

For both of them, Neil and Toni, the perfect answer would have been a flat of their own but neither of them had any real idea how to go about acquiring one. The medical social worker at the hospital obtained forms from the Petersfield Housing Department and these had been duly filled in and posted back, but for the time being a return to Steep was the only option. For Neil, in particular, it was an appalling dilemma. On the one hand he was genuinely grateful for his family's support, especially when he'd seen the consequences of what could happen to people without it, but on the other hand, he was still the Neil Slatter who'd been on the verge of leaving home. None of the old desires — for freedom, money, travel — had died, and in his more frivolous moments he was tempted to regard his tetraplegia as simply a minor hiccough, a local difficulty, a purely mechanical handicap to be overcome before he resumed his journey to wherever it might take him. But deep down he was realistic enough to know that life had changed utterly, and that most of his former objectives were now pipe dreams. In one sense that wasn't such a bad thing. Inside himself, he was already aware of profound changes, an abrupt transition from adolescence to something far quieter, more reflective, less painful. Whether that peace would survive the inevitable pressures of life at Steep was anyone's guess, but for the time being there was simply no alternative.

As with everything else at Stoke Mandeville, going home is a gradual affair. Patients' progress at physio and OT sessions is carefully monitored until the doctors judge that it's time for a trial weekend away. This first taste of life outside will be the forerunner of a number of similar weekends before the patient leaves for good, and it's precisely at this point that relatives become as important to the hospital as patients.

Prior to the first weekend, relatives are invited up to Stoke Mandeville where they stay overnight in a specially provided mobile home. The evening they spend on the ward, watching carefully while every detail of the nightly routine is explained. The following morning they return, learning about bed baths, manual bowel evacuations, bladder care, transfers from bed to wheelchair, and the vital daily checks for incipient pressure sores. For staff like Sister Rose, the relatives' reactions are extremely important. "A lot of the women have been mothers of course, and they simply become mothers again. They think they'll never be able to make it, but they cope marvellously. Some, of course, don't cope. They say straight away it won't work and they ask at once for alternative arrangements".

In Neil's case, there were no such qualms. Eileen had already picked up a good deal from her regular weekends at Stoke Mandeville, while Toni had become an expert in the care of the chronically disabled. Nevertheless, Eileen remembers how nervous she was. "I just knew how important it was not to fail him and I was just hoping I was strong enough and clever enough to get it all right. When we were leaving the ward they all made a great fuss of him, and then one of the doctors took me aside and told me it would be at least five years before anyone could tell how he was really coping. "We've done as much as we can…" he said to me, "… from now on everything's a bonus".

Chapter Five

It was winter by the time Neil made his first expedition back to Steep. The Stoke Mandeville weekend runs from Friday afternoon to Sunday evening, and on the Friday Eileen had set off from Petersfield in mid-morning to arrive at Stoke just after lunch. With luck, Neil would be back home before nightfall.

At Steep, Bob and Eileen had done their best to prepare the cottage for Neil's return. Handicapped by a lack of space, they'd first planned to give Neil one of the two upstairs bedrooms. This would mean installing a lift on the stairs, an adaptation which is normally funded by the DHSS, but when officials called to make an inspection they decided that the staircase was too narrow to permit the installation of any of the available models. That meant that Neil would have to live downstairs in the single living room.

This room occupied most of the ground floor. It had already been extended once, and at the far end a door opened into a small timber conservatory, and then into the garden. Even with the extension, the living room wasn't big, and Eileen had spent many evenings trying to decide how best to divide the space. With the addition of Toni and Neil, the room would have to contain four separate lives — and Eileen was all too conscious that Neil's well-being depended on a little privacy, as well as the provision of every other need. In the end she'd solved the problem by dividing the room in half with a curtain. Beyond the curtain, Bob had installed one of the Bedales dormitory beds, specially heightened with blocks to make for easier nursing, and he'd also built a concrete ramp from the conservatory to provide Neil with access to the garden. A folding sun lounger gave Toni a bed beside Neil, and the rest of the room was rearranged to make Neil its focal point. Life would be unavoidably intimate, but with luck and a great deal of mutual forbearance, the arrangement might just work.

For Neil, the prospect of his first weekend at home meant a curious mixture of apprehension and excitement. He was keen to sample the nearly forgotten pleasures of the real world — fresh air, beer, old friends — but he was profoundly aware of how much he'd come to depend on the hospital regime. Tetraplegics have a highly developed need for physical security, and while life on Ward One X had its limitations, it was comforting to know that help was never more than a few seconds away. Home was a lovely thought, but what would happen if things went wrong?

Eileen and Bob arrived at Stoke Mandeville just after lunch and Toni pushed Neil's wheelchair out into the thin November sunlight. Eileen remembers trying to contain a sense of excitement which had been mounting all week, but this quickly evaporated. "It was strange. I'd got really excited about Neil coming home and I somehow thought he'd suddenly look healthy again, like the old Neil, but he didn't. He was very anxious, very nervous, and he had that awful hospital pallor that people get when they've been in bed too long. All he wanted to do was to get home as soon as possible."

Out in the car park Neil's first problem was getting into the car. The technique most commonly used for transfers of tetraplegics from a wheelchair to a car is called the standing lift. A relative or friend removes the footplates from the wheelchair and then positions the chair alongside the open passenger door. In this case it was Toni. With the chair beside the car, she then stood in front of Neil with her feet either side of his, bent down towards him, and slid her hands, palms upwards, beneath his buttocks. Neil put his arms round her neck and came up out of the wheelchair as she unbent. With both of them upright, Toni then swivelled Neil round and lowered him into the car seat where Eileen tied him down like a parcel with the safety belts. To watching passers-by, the manoeuvre looked awkward, almost grotesque, Toni dwarfed by the sagging bulk of Neil's body but however inelegant, it worked.

With Neil safely strapped into the front passenger seat, the four of them set off on the ninety mile journey back to Steep, Eileen driving and Toni and Bob in the back of the tiny Datsun. With the hospital behind them, Eileen was cheerful again, but at the first roundabout it became obvious that their troubles were far from over. As the car turned left into the roundabout, Neil's fourteen and a half stone swayed to the right and only the safety belt prevented him from collapsing altogether onto Eileen. Eileen fended him off for long enough to join the traffic flow around the island, but as soon as the car began to go right, Neil's body obeyed the momentum of the turn and slid across the seat towards the door. Unrestrained by the seat belt, his head crashed into the window, an impact which left him in no doubt about the sensitivity of his few remaining nerves.

Out of the roundabout, Eileen stopped the car, and for the next few minutes she and Toni experimented with a combination of seat belts and cushions until Neil was wedged securely upright. Thus protected from further mishap, the four of them completed the two and a half hour journey, Toni supplying a precautionary arm on all but the gentlest of bends. For Eileen, in particular, it was an abrupt introduction to the real implications of caring for her newly tetraplegic son. "On the way up to Stoke Mandeville I remember seeing a tree or a particular view or something and making a little mental note thinking we'd stop there on the way back and I'd be able to show him but, of course, once we'd sorted him out in the car he didn't want to stop. He had his neck collar on and we'd tightened the seat belts as much as we dared but even so I drove like a nun. I was even frightened of going over matchsticks. The journey seemed to take forever and by the time we got him back, all he wanted to do was to go to bed".

Safely back at Steep, Neil did his best to mask the initial disappointments of this first expedition home. All around him was the evidence of his former life — books, records, the family spaniel, his guitar — but everything was now qualified by the fact of his own impotence. Not only did he depend entirely on others for movement, food and warmth, but he was all too conscious of the contrast between the efficient routines of Ward One X and the well-intentioned semi-chaos of Dunhill Mews. "Being at home for the first time was very nerve racking for everyone. I'd been used to everything running very smoothly and of course, at home it wasn't at all like that and that would make me very nervous and irritable. Things like condoms going. You'd just get into the Cricketers or some other pub and — bang — it would go and we'd have to go back home. I think the most nervous person those weekends was Eileen because she knew just how much was expected from her."

For her part, Eileen now admits to feelings which often verged on near panic. "I think we all realised that having Neil home would be no picnic. I know I was terrified of making mistakes. It was so important not to fail him."

These obvious qualms apart, this and subsequent trial weekends at Steep passed off moderately well. The days were all too brief, and Neil's presence was all too novel, to permit any real tension — and Eileen, fiercely maternal, was delighted to have her son back under the

Toni performs a standing chair lift to get Neil into a car. Her legs act as a brace for his.

family roof. For Neil too, there were real compensations for his anxieties about becoming the guinea pig in a crash course in tetraplegic nursing. Eileen's cooking was a welcome change from hospital food, and Sunday lunchtime outings to the pub reminded him that there was still a life to explore and enjoy.

More than that, though, Neil became abruptly aware that he was gazing out at the world through very different eyes. Once, on a Saturday afternoon, he was packed into the car and driven fifteen miles down the A3 to Southsea where Bob parked on the seafront. "That was really nice. Having been so close to death, I was suddenly conscious of looking at everything anew. Very simple things — colours, clouds, seagulls — meant the whole world to me. I really appreciated them. Then things that we all take for granted become fascinating. I'd sit there in the car watching people walking by and I'd think how marvellous it all was, just the sheer act of walking and keeping your balance, because I knew how bloody hard those things were. You can't ever have that kind of feeling unless you've been through something like Stoke Mandeville. Unless you're a cripple, you take the whole lot for granted."

Patients at Stoke Mandeville normally have perhaps a dozen weekends away before the final break with the hospital but the imminence of Christmas that year meant — for Neil — an earlier departure than usual. The medical staff were also impressed by Toni's competence. Four months on Ward One X had taught her a great deal about the care of tetraplegics, and this experience would give Neil a flying start in his new life outside. On the 14th December 1977, Neil was finally discharged from Stoke Mandeville.

But back at Steep, things went quickly wrong. Neil just had time to enjoy a noisy, crowded Christmas before he was hit with a bladder infection. Bladder infections can be a regular curse for the spinally injured. A large intake of fluid, as much as five pints a day, helps to flush the system through, but even this is no guarantee of immunity. In itself, a bladder infection may not be serious, but above the bladder lie the kidneys — the key to the body's ability to filter impurities from the blood — and if infection spreads to these delicate organs, the consequences can be permanent. Thus the need to treat serious bladder infections as quickly as possible.

For Neil, the symptoms were a familiar — if depressing — throwback to his months at Stoke where bladder infections were all too routine. He woke up one morning with a headache. His urine was cloudy. Not as much was passing as usual. It smelt awful. He developed a temperature. He began to sweat. Toni knew at once what was wrong and telephoned the GP who arrived within the hour. He confirmed a bladder infection and Toni waited for him to perform a catheterisation, a routine procedure for draining the bladder. On this occasion, though, the GP decided against performing the catheterisation that seemed to be required. It was, he felt, a decision for the specialists. Toni and Neil glanced at each other. Specialists meant Stoke Mandeville, and within half a day Neil was packed into the back of an ambulance and returned to Stoke. The infection itself was thankfully minor and treatment took only a couple of days, but the episode was doubly significant: for one thing it reminded Neil that the line between hospital and home was extremely thin, and for another it was the most graphic evidence that large parts of the medical establishment knew very little about spinal injury.

As with all paraplegics and tetraplegics, Neil's relationship with his GP was extremely important. Now, years later, there's a great deal of give and take but in the early stages his GP was understandably reluctant to admit his own lack of specialist knowledge or to accept that Neil or Toni were trustworthy sources of advice. Unlike sufferers from other conditions, the spinally injured are encouraged to take as much interest in their own treatment as possible, and over the long months of hospital care they build up an impressive expertise. They learn to avoid certain postures, certain foods, recognise certain symptoms, and relate these to specific treatments. For the best possible motive — their own survival — they therefore become qualified in the management of their own conditions. Given the cautious attentions of a GP who may never have seen a paraplegic in his life, it's small wonder that the relationship between patient and doctor can become extremely difficult. With time, the relationship normally settles down. Neil's GP now accepts that Neil himself is an excellent judge of his own condition and is an enormous help in the establishment of a diagnosis. But in the early days at Steep, this incident was the first real evidence of a world which was either unwilling or unable to accept the full implications of tetraplegia.

Newly discharged from Stoke, Neil returned once again to the family cottage at Steep where life began to settle into a recognisable routine. Toni and Eileen had already sorted out their various areas of responsibility and although the compromise between them was far from perfect, it seemed to work. Eileen was still employed as an auxiliary at the local geriatric hospital but daily adjustments to her shifts meant that she could still fit in the housework and the cooking as well. This left Toni with sole responsibility for the care of Neil, a job for which she was now well qualified, but the very fact that this should fall exclusively to Toni and to no one else left its mark on Eileen. Neil was, after all, her son — and it was sometimes difficult to accept that he seemed to have become the physical property of someone else. ''I actually got on very well with Toni. We all loved her and treated her as part of the family but it was quite hard sometimes. Deep down I wanted to do everything for Neil and occasionally I'd get a bit fed up and wonder why it was me having to go out and earn the money and do all the housework all the time, and not Toni."

For her part, Toni also had her qualms. For the first time she was beginning to realise the full implications of looking after someone as badly handicapped as Neil. For five months at Stoke Mandeville she'd sat patiently at his bedside, devoting herself as completely as possible to getting him out of hospital and back to Steep. Now, without the help of doctors, nurses, physios, occupational therapists, and the small army of other specialists on call at Stoke, she was on her own. The long-term implications frightened her and most of the time she preferred to shut her eyes to the future, but her own peace of mind demanded some kind of long-term plan, some faint notion of where it all might lead. "I knew there was no choice for the time being but it was very important to me to have a future of my own and when I really got down to it there was no doubt what I had to do: regardless of what Neil wanted, I was determined to make him as independent as possible in order to give me enough peace of mind to be able — one day — to leave. That didn't mean I didn't love him. In a way, I did. But in the end I had to be sure I'd be able to make my own decisions, and live my own life. Anything else would have killed me."

In the short term though, there was simply an endless list of jobs to be done, and as the days went by she began to fit the theories she'd learned at Stoke to the practice of coping at Steep, a process which often had its funnier side. "Hilarious, the things we did wrong. We had a big list of dos and don'ts from the hospital and Eileen was very keen on the rules — she wanted to do the best for Neil, obviously — but it wasn't that easy in the mornings. I had to fit the condoms on him. That meant holding his penis straight and then spreading this glue from a tube. Often I'd put too much on, and then get the condom on the wrong way, inside out, so it wouldn't roll, then by the time I'd sorted all that out, all the glue would have trickled down to the bottom where it made a terrible mess. You can imagine. Then everyone would gather round, a great committee, all making suggestions, all trying to help. It can't have been much fun for Neil but he was very resigned. I suppose under the circumstances he didn't have a lot of choice."

Another daily test was getting Neil dressed. "Putting his clothes on was a joke, like trying to dress something with no bones in it. When I was putting on shirts or a pullover, I'd hold him up with one arm while

I tried to get him into the thing with the other. He weighed a ton, of course, and little things like his hand locked at right angles to his wrist meant the sleeves took forever. The hardest part was his feet. The hospital told us to use soft shoes, like baseball boots, to cut down the chance of pressure sores, but they were as floppy as the rest of him, so in the end I gave up and used proper leather boots which were rigid. That made it much easier. Putting his trousers on was a nightmare. In hospital they teach you a kind of rolling technique, where you roll him onto one side, then the other, while you inch the trousers up his leg, one bit at a time. But this took forever, too, so in the end I used to lie him on the bed on his back, flex both legs, pull the trousers half way up his thighs, then whizz round the back of him and heave him off the bed, pulling hard on the trousers at the same time. That used to do the trick. Another bright idea the hospital taught us was to sew a 'V' of material into the top of all his trouser seams. This was supposed to ease the pressure and make everything looser, but the problem there was that once his trousers were on, and he was upright, they simply fell down, leaving him with his bum hanging out. Neil didn't particularly care about that because everything was new and I think he was very conscious of what he'd become. He didn't really want to go out or anything. But I cared. I wasn't having him looking a shambles. So I started getting him back into real trousers."

The whole question of what Neil should wear became something of an issue between the two women. Eileen, ever mindful of hospital advice, provided a seemingly endless supply of oversize pullovers and specially adapted shirts. The latter had draw strings fitted round the hem at the bottom. In theory this was supposed to keep the shirts in place around his belly, but in practice the shirts simply rode up, much to Toni's annoyance. The more she saw of other disabled people, the more she was determined that Neil would look as normal as possible — not just for appearances sake, but for his long-term peace of mind. Wearing special clothes, eating special diets, and all the other concessions to recommended tetraplegic behaviour, were just part and parcel of a slow surrender to the *idea* of being a cripple. It was pointless pretending that Neil was physically normal, but it did him no favours to treat him like some kind of freak, to be protected and cossetted and generally put to one side. To make a stand against this kind of apartheid was by no means easy because Neil was given every incentive to step into the box marked 'Cripple'. That, at least, was the way Toni saw it. 'Think of the tools they gave him at the hospital. First of all he had these leather things that fitted over his hand. They had special slots on the palm side: one for his spoon, one for his fork, one for his toothbrush. They'd all been specially measured and made in the OT Department. Then he had special sticky mats to put under his plate at mealtimes to stop the stuff slopping around. And there were special guards to fit round the edges of plates. So any time we ever went anywhere, all this gear had to come with us in a carrier bag. It was like going round with a baby. I hated it from the start but I don't think it really dawned on Neil until he saw another cripple eating. That really shook him. It looked so embarrassing. It just underlined what he'd become. He said he'd prefer to go hungry rather than depend on them forever."

Aware that Neil needed company, as well as non-stop care, Eileen did her best to encourage Neil's old friends to drop in. Many took up the invitation, staying for a meal or drinks, sitting in a semi-circle round Neil with the hi-fi up and the room thick with smoke while Bob and Eileen beat a discreet retreat upstairs to the relative peace of their tiny bedroom. One of the early arrivals was Keith Wilde, one of Neil's oldest buddies, whom Toni now met for the first time. He'd already been up to Stoke and knew that Neil bore no visible scars from the accident, but the scene at Dunhill Mews still took him by surprise. "It was amazing. It was as if he'd never left. There he was, lying on the sofa, while all the women in the Slatter family — Eileen, Toni, and Hilda and Emma (Neil's sisters-in-law) fussed around him. It was perfect. Exactly his set up. He was king again".

With time and company at his disposal, Neil renewed a lifelong interest in cards, a pastime to which he'd now introduced Toni. In hospital they'd been limited to the simpler games. Now she watched him becoming more ambitious. "Things like rummy were OK because they didn't involve more than about seven cards. He could just about cope with that between his thumb and first finger and then he'd use his teeth to select a card — though close up he'd often make a mistake and pull out the wrong one and that would make him mad. But after a while he got a craze for Canasta, and that went over the top. You play with two packs and there were cards everywhere, all over him."

On many evenings the games and music and conversation lasted until well past midnight. At that point, the house would empty, leaving Toni the job of manhandling Neil back into bed. The hospital had recommended that Neil was to be turned every three hours as a precaution against pressure sores, and so Toni's evening always ended with the setting of an alarm clock before she could unfold her sun lounger and risk a few hours sleep. Many nights, Neil found it impossible to sleep at all, and on these occasions Toni would sit up with him, reading aloud from the latest sci-fi novel or simply talking.

Other times, once Eileen and Bob had retired for the night, they tried to piece together the beginnings of a mutually satisfying sex life. They'd discussed the possibilities at Stoke, but now there was a chance to put their theories to the test. In a letter to the GP, Neil's Stoke Mandeville specialist had described his remaining sexual capability as "reflex erection only", but Neil was far from deterred. "Sexually he got quite ambitious but it was all a bit of a procedure. First of all I had to get all his gear off — the condom and the tube to his leg bag and so forth — then I had to take advantage of his erection before it went because it wasn't very long lasting. Then because I was on top of him bouncing up and down he tended to wet himself — but however messy it was he'd just battle on because he had so much to prove. Later it got much better because he got so much more relaxed about it all. But the whole thing must have been terrible for him then because there he'd been — able bodied and sexed up to the eyebrows and into everything that moved — and suddenly, bang, nothing."

Apart from meeting Neil's need for company, Eileen was also concerned about the lack of regular physio. The social services provide a network of visiting physios across the country but a lack of funds meant that there were none available for the Petersfield district. Toni did her best to fill in, and she'd spend many hours carefully exercising Neil's fingers, one after the other, in a bid to keep them supple. But it wasn't quite the same as formal physio and Eileen finally solved the problem by asking the GP to refer Neil to a local orthopaedic centre where elderly patients from her own hospital paid frequent visits.

The new hospital, the Lord Mayor Treloar at Alton, agreed to accept Neil one day a week, and every Tuesday Eileen and Bob would pack Neil into the car and drive the fifteen miles to Alton where he received the attentions of trained physios. They kept his joints and muscles supple with mat work and weight routines, and the climax to the day's therapy was a session in the hydro-therapy pool, an irregular shaped warm water bath about the size of the average living room. Water is an ideal medium for physiotherapy because of the support it gives the muscles, and Neil would be strapped into a flotation collar and lowered into the water by means of a special hoist. In the water, he'd be joined by two physios who'd exercise various parts of his body, and he'd end the session with a couple of widths of the pool. Strictly speaking, these were against regulations but the physios turned a blind eye while Neil's collar was detached and he took as deep a breath as his remaining muscles permitted. Turned face down in the water, he'd then paddle himself to the opposite side of the pool where another attendant would be waiting to turn him face up. To the onlooker it was a strangely pathetic sight, but for Neil it had all the makings of a glorious achievement.

The weekly trips to Alton weren't the only excursions. The more thoughtful of Neil's friends sometimes volunteered to push him the half mile down the hill to The Cricketers where he'd once worked as a barman. There, he got a mixed reception. "Some people couldn't cope. I don't know why but they took one look at the wheelchair and didn't want to know. That made me feel awful, more on their behalf than mine. But others saw me and not my wheelchair, and that mattered a lot."

Another trip, more ambitious, was to the local cinema in Petersfield, called The Savoy. Neil had noticed a film he wanted to see in the local paper and Eileen had encouraged them both to have an evening out. A taxi was duly ordered, but when it turned up the driver refused to take the wheelchair. Words were exchanged on the subject and by the time the driver had gone, still adamant that wheelchairs weren't his responsibility, the film had started. Underterred, Eileen ordered a different taxi for the following night, this time taking the precaution of discussing the wheelchair on the phone. The taxi arrived on time, the wheelchair was packed into the boot, and Toni and Neil set off for the Savoy.

On arrival Toni got out of the taxi first. "I stood there on the pavement for a bit getting the wheelchair ready but there was no question of anyone giving me a hand to get Neil out of the taxi. There were people everywhere but they just stood there and watched. Then I went up to the women at the kiosk and asked for two tickets but she refused. She said they didn't want "his sort" in the cinema. She obviously thought he was insane. She wouldn't talk to Neil. She'd only talk to me. At this point I got really wild but Neil stayed very calm and asked to see the manager. The woman was astonished. The cripple actually talked. The manager, though, wasn't around. The woman said he was only on the end of a telephone. So Neil talked to him on the phone and he said it was a question of fire regulations. Wheelchairs weren't allowed in because of the fire risk. We could only go in if Neil was transferred to a seat. If he was serious about the fire risk, this was daft because Neil would never have been able to get out in time, but that's the way they wanted it. We kept on at them and told them about a particular row at the back where a seat had been removed which would have been perfect for Neil's chair but they insisted on a transfer. It was unbelievable."

Barred entry to the cinema, Toni and Neil retreated to Steep once again. Eileen was furious and next day she mentioned the incident to Paul Wickham, a local publican and a good friend of Neil's. He was outraged and in turn contacted Elsa Bulmer, then Mayor of Petersfield, who agreed at once to get help in any way she could. She already knew the consequences of tetraplegia in the shape of Danny Hearn, a rugby-playing friend who'd broken his neck during an England/All Blacks International match in 1967. Danny had been a housemaster at Haileybury during her son's school days, and the way he'd coped with the aftermath of the injury had made a permanent impression. Faced with this latest evidence of society's knack of heaping insults on injury, she contacted the District Council's Chief Executive and investigated the possibilities of redrafting the cinema's licence to make life more comfortable for people like Neil. Her efforts in this direction finally came to very little, but she was never in doubt about the principles involved in hiding behind fire regulations. "It just seemed so morally wrong. I felt that if we were to try and cocoon the disabled, to eliminate the element of risk altogether, then they'd cease to be human beings."

In the aftermath of the Savoy incident, life at Dunhill Mews became grimmer. Quiet, introspective, and increasingly depressed, Neil began to spend more and more time in bed. One of the practical reasons for this retreat was the discovery that he was developing a pressure sore. An awkward transfer from the car to the wheelchair had bruised the base of Neil's spine. Eileen and Toni kept a careful eye on this patch of bruising, and when it began to become reddened they called in the GP. Because of its position, the bruise was highly vulnerable to further damage of which Neil would be entirely unaware, and so the GP advised that Neil should spend more of his day in bed. This Neil did, only too conscious that the consequences of the bruise turning into a real pressure sore would be yet another spell in Stoke Mandeville.

But bed depressed him. After months of looking forward to getting out of hospital and back to some semblance of real life, he was horizontal again and totally at the mercy of other people. Unprepared to be simply a passive recipient of other people's favours, he began to lash out, a reaction all the more violent for its obvious physical limitations.

To Eileen, especially, he was constantly spiteful, driving her from the house by the force of his resentment. "Toni and I used to go on long walks through the woods and commiserate together. I think it was frustration more than anything because Neil can be very pig-headed, and I think he was frightened too. But at least I could get out to work. For Toni, there was no escape, and Neil just got lower and lower because he knew he wasn't getting any better. The contrast with Stoke Mandeville must have been terrible. We were fumblers compared to the professionals".

Toni, too, came in for her share of abuse, and it was often difficult not to retaliate. "It was easy to hate Neil in those early days because he could be so vicious. In the hospital it didn't matter. I wrote it off. He was ill. Forget it. But at home it was very different. Once he'd decided it wasn't worth getting up, the entire house had to revolve around him. He wouldn't bloody move so we had to go to him. Just to make it bearable, we'd form little alliances against him. 'God, isn't he impossible', we'd say. He even began to get through to Bob".

By this time it was obvious even to Eileen that the attempt to look after Neil at home, to somehow build a bridge between his own needs and ordinary life, was failing. The cottage was simply too small to let two couples — different ages, different needs — co-exist, and so Eileen turned her attention to the Housing Department in the hope that some form of council accommodation might be found. Neil and Toni's application from Stoke Mandeville had by now landed on the Petersfield desk of David Hooper, a Housing Department official charged with special responsibility for the district's disabled. Petersfield had already acquired a good reputation for looking after its disabled and had been one of the first local authorities to respond to sections of the 1974 Housing Act which empowered councils to make special provision for the disabled. A block of flats had been built, with a number of units set aside for the disabled, and at first the council had been unable to find enough tenants. But four years later there was a longish waiting list and David Hooper now saw little possibility of an immediate offer.

In January 1978, after Neil had returned from Stoke Mandeville, David Hooper had gone up to the cottage at Steep to meet him and even then — before the onset of the pressure sore — he'd been moved by the sight of the young tetraplegic lying in bed in the downstairs living room sipping orange juice through a straw. The place felt cold, the atmosphere was depressing, and of all the disabled he'd met, he thought that Neil was "the worst off". At the end of that first meeting, he'd promised to investigate the possibilities of a ground floor flat on a new council estate at Froxfield, a small village a couple of miles up the road, and this prospect had raised Neil's hopes. But as the weeks went by, and there was no word from David Hooper, his spirits sank lower and lower until a cold dark morning in March when the phone rang and David came through to say that the Froxfield flat had fallen through. In retrospect Froxfield would have been a disaster. It was miles from anywhere and had few facilities. But at the time it represented the only way out of Steep — and for Neil Steep was fast becoming a nightmare. "At the time we'd pinned all our hopes on it and when the phone call came in and Toni told me that the flat had fallen through it was the end of everything. I remember nearly breaking down. That was one of the lowest points."

With Neil plunging ever deeper into depression and the pressure sore showing every sign of getting worse, Eileen and Toni once again called on Elsa Bulmer who came up to Steep to see Neil for herself. Like David Hooper, she found him silent and resigned. "He was very, very quiet, very depressed. I think life was becoming unbearable for him. I think that particular period was very critical. Wonderful as his parents were, it simply wasn't working. He could easily have gone under."

For Neil, things could scarcely get worse, but it was precisely at this point that he had yet another official visitation, this time in the shape of two pleasant young men from the Disabled Rehabilitation Office, charged with assessing his suitability for work. Under the 1944 Disabled Persons Employment Act, the Government established a Register for the disabled. The Act stipulates that every firm employing more than twenty people has an obligation to make sure that at least 3 per cent of its workforce are Registered Disabled, though dispensations can be obtained by application to Disabled Rehabilitation Officers (DROs). In theory, the Act was originally supposed to guarantee post-war employment for Britain's disabled ex-servicemen, but in practice the Register has now lost credibility — both with employers who claim that there aren't enough qualified disabled to go round, and with the disabled themselves who've lost faith in the Government's willingness to enforce the Act and therefore don't bother to register in the first place.

The two young men who arrived with their clipboards at Steep that morning had come to see Neil, who still has vivid memories of what happened next. "I was lying there in bed but they wouldn't talk to me. Only Toni. Finally they got through all their questions and said they'd be able to send me away on a two-month training course and after that I'd be able to fit shower heads to shower pipes. Toni asked them what would happen to us, our personal relationship, and that was their first shock because we weren't really allowed to have a personal relationship. Then I spoke up for the first time and said that I wanted to become an accountant and that really threw them. They scuttled off and never once came back."

By this time, winter was coming to an end but as the days lengthened, Neil's pressure sore took a turn for the worse. The redness had by this time turned a darker shade and broken open into an ulcer. The GP made regular visits and on his advice the District Nurse began to pack the sore with sterile dressings. Every day, it seemed, the cavity got a little wider and a little deeper, placing even greater restrictions on Neil. By now he'd virtually given up leaving the house and his only concession to fresh air was to let Toni and Eileen push the bed out through the conservatory and into the garden where he was able to enjoy a couple of days of early spring sunshine. There he'd lie in bed, supported on pillows beneath the shade of a protective umbrella conducting the odd conversation with passing pupils from Bedales who used a path at the bottom of the garden as a short cut between two parts of the school.

During this period, Neil's condition was frequently complicated by further bladder infections, partly because the regular removal of the condom was playing havoc with his penis, and partly because he wasn't drinking the recommended five pints of liquid a day. It was Toni's job to try and relieve the almost constant discomfort. "First of all I'd lie him on his back on the bed. The bladder was often so swollen you could actually see it. Then I'd hit the bladder again and again, just to try and stir it into action. Sometimes I'd press down on it really hard, hard enough to be able to feel his backbone, and this would often work, and stuff would come out through the condom, but it also caused him terrible indigestion-type pains in the chest and he'd scream and scream but it was the only way. The doctor used to prescribe Valium to help him sleep and I used to get so upset about him suffering so much that I'd give him a double dose. Once Eileen and I were in the living room and Neil was in bed, out of it all on a double dose, and quite suddenly he stopped breathing. I just didn't know what to do. I thought he'd simply start again but nothing happened. Then I told Eileen and she was marvellous. She just got him up in bed and doubled him over, just like you do with babies, and it worked. Thank God she was there. I was just panicking. I didn't know what to do. I never told her about the double dose, but I did tell Neil, later, when he'd come round. I don't think he really believed me. He couldn't remember anything, of course, so in a sense it didn't matter."

As March gave way to April, the sore got worse. By this time it was

69

about the size of a penny, at the top of the cleft between Neil's buttocks, a position which left Neil literally wide open to infection from the twice weekly manual evacuations when either Toni or Eileen would empty his bowels. On hospital advice, Neil was still taking regular doses of a laxative called Dorbanex, and the resulting faeces were far from solid. Not only was this distressing for Neil, whose sense of smell was far from impaired, but the stuff also had a tendency to obey gravity, trickling down the channel between his buttocks towards the ulcerated pressure sore. Regardless of how many times the District Nurse cleaned out the sore it was therefore bound to reinfect. After a while it got deeper still, until Eileen became seriously alarmed. "I knew about pressure sores because Heathside, the geriatric hospital where I worked, was full of them, but they seemed to get better. Neil's didn't. The packing that went in every day just got deeper and deeper. We thought maybe the dressings weren't sterile so we did it ourselves. But it was very hard. Everything had to be boiled. There was endless treatment."

At this point, ironically, David Hooper arrived with the offer of a council flat — not at Froxfield, but down in Petersfield on a council estate to the south of the town. The flat was entirely unadapted but it was on the ground floor and the estate as a whole was within pushing distance from the centre of Petersfield.

On the 10th May, Liz Hardley, Toni and Eileen went to look at the flat. Liz Hardley was an Occupational Therapist based at Alton who looked after a huge slice of south-east Hampshire, and it was her job to offer Toni a professional assessment of which adaptations might make life easier. Together, the three women toured the empty flat. There was a door at the front which opened into a narrow hall, and another door at the side which provided access to the kitchen. Both entrances had steps, a major obstacle for a wheelchair. Inside there were six rooms, including two bedrooms. Furniture was non-existent and the only heating came from an open fire in the living room. Both Toni and Eileen were now experienced enough to be able to recognise the obvious drawbacks from Neil's point of view, but it was Liz Hardley who turned their remarks into a shopping list of alterations which she was soon to send to David Hooper.

First there was the critical problem of access. Not only must a new door be opened into the house to give Toni a chance of getting Neil's wheelchair in and out, but there were also problems inside. The house had been built for the able bodied. Passageways were narrow and corners tight. Most critical of all were the bathroom and toilet facilities.

Only by knocking down the wall between them, and widening the doorway would Toni have a chance of manoeuvering Neil in and out.

There was also the question of the bath. Getting Neil in and out of a bath would be a physical impossibility, while a shower would make washing his body relatively simple. Liz therefore suggested that the bath be removed and a shower installed in its place. The shower should include a thermostatic unit to control the temperature of the water and thus spare Neil needless scalds.

Finally, there was the question of heating for the flat. In May the place felt reasonably warm but in winter it would be a different matter. Tetraplegics like Neil are quite unable to feel cold over the majority of their body surface, but the physiological effects are just the same. An ordinary cold can easily develop into bronchitis or even pneumonia. Liz Hardley therefore ended her list with a request for central heating. With that, the three women completed their tour, agreeing that Toni and Neil should take possession of the flat as soon as possible.

Days later, in mid-May, Toni and Neil left Steep and moved down to Grange Road. The bed at Dunhill Mews was packed up and returned to Bedales, and Bob retrieved the family furniture from the spare bedroom upstairs. Their practical support for Neil was still enormous — they were both down at Grange Road every day — but the real responsibility now rested with Toni. Toni, though, was far from happy. The pressure sore had gone from bad to worse, and she knew enough about rudimentary nursing to recognise the smell of gangrene. "At that point I disowned responsibility for it and got the doctor back in. He said to swab it down with Eusol (a disinfectant) every day to clean it out. The District Nurse used to come in and do that but it was so close to his anus that the thing kept reinfecting again. The flesh just went grey and slimy and the smell was terrible, like rotting meat, and every day we'd go deeper and deeper. Then one morning I fished out a piece of bone from the bottom of the spine. I phoned up the GP and told him what I'd found but he wasn't impressed. Next day I found a bit more so this time I popped it into one finger of the evac glove and took it round to show him. He was appalled. It was bone after all..."

Later that day, the GP dialled an Aylesbury number. It was June. Within twenty four hours, Neil was back at Stoke Mandeville.

Chapter Six

Neil returned to Stoke Mandeville on the 29th June 1978 for his second summer in hospital. This time, though, it was different. Gone was the feeling of bewilderment, of not knowing what was happening and why, and in its place was something far closer to resignation. From the purely medical point of view the case for readmission was overwhelming. Neil knew enough about pressure sores, and about gangrene, to realise that the consequences could easily be fatal, and the fact that Stoke could find room for him at twenty four hours notice was itself a reassurance. The only question left worth asking was how long he'd have to stay.

Pressure sores occur when the supply of life-giving blood is cut off from a particular area of the body. Denied blood, the flesh will die. Normally, incipient pressure sores signal themselves as discomfort and our response — a movement of the body — is enough to relieve the pressure and re-establish the blood supply. But the spinally injured lack these warning signs, and with the flesh dead or dying infection can quickly set in, a process which often begins near the bone.

In Neil's case, the pressure sore was well established and the doctors' first task was to get rid of the infection which was slowly eating his flesh away. Every day the open wound was cleaned out and freshly dressed, and swabs were taken at regular intervals for analysis in the hospital's laboratory. The results of these tests told the doctors whether or not the infection had cleared up, and only when successive swabs showed no infection would the consultant consider his next step. In the meantime, Neil was obliged to lie flat in the prone position supported on a bed of carefully positioned pillows. Every three hours his body would be turned to prevent fresh pressure sores developing on the front or flanks of his body, and he also received regular visits from physios and occupational therapists. Flat on his belly he was once again at the mercy of the Stoke Mandeville healing machine.

His surroundings, though, were different from his first spell at Stoke. This time he'd been assigned to Three X, a ward containing re-admissions. For this reason his fellow patients tended to be older, more experienced men, some of whom had half a lifetime of disability behind them. Their outlook and attitudes were a marked contrast to the anxious bravado of Ward One X, and over the following months Neil was to develop the beginnings of a new relationship towards his tetraplegia. In the long term he'd be able to view this as a turning point, a bonus, but for the time being it was simply another open-ended period of helplessness and uncertainty. Until the swabs began to give negative results, there were simply no promises to be made.

Back at Petersfield, both Toni and Eileen were able to breath a sigh of relief. In one sense the move to Grange Road had already removed Eileen's major responsibility, but she'd become seriously disturbed by the state of the pressure sore and sensed that it was time to admit defeat and hand Neil back to the doctors. "Toni and I were just so glad that he was back there and safe again. Somehow there wasn't the fear this time. It wasn't a broken neck any more. It was a pressure sore. So it wasn't the unknown this time. We knew what to expect, we knew the people, and it was doing Toni good as well because she had the freedom."

For Toni, freedom was a novel experience. For the first time in twelve months she was spared the daily responsibility of looking after Neil. In hospital, for the first five months, she'd tried to keep his mind together while the doctors did their best with the rest of him; at Steep and at Grange Road, she'd had to cope by herself. Eileen had certainly been a help. She'd done the cooking and helped with the heavier tasks and generally kept the house running round the pair of them, but the weeks that she and Neil spent together at Grange Road had been enough to give her a depressing taste of what could easily amount to the rest of her life. The flat had been cold, cheerless and awkward, and a series of chilly evenings had given her an unsettling preview of what the autumn and winter would be like. It had been difficult moving Neil from room to room, and getting him out of the house had depended on help from Bob, his father, who lived several miles away. Liz Hardley, the visiting occupational therapist, had assured her that alterations were in hand but nothing that Toni had seen of the workings of local government convinced her that the promises would be kept. Council committees took a long time to make up their minds. There were so many people involved. Money was tight. And builders — once contracted — were notoriously slow.

Just thinking about the long chain of form filling, visits, assessments, and re-assessments made her tired — and attending to Neil's physical needs, though now routine, was no less demanding. True, Neil and Eileen had suggested a Home Help, but Toni viewed a stranger in the house as marginally worse than exhaustion and had turned the offer down. It was her job to get Neil better, and that she would tackle alone. But there'd been no improvement. On the contrary he'd gone from bad to worse until he refused to get out of bed at all, and their lives had revolved almost entirely around the television. They'd start viewing in the morning, watch through the endless sequence of cartoons, quiz games, women's shows, and kids programmes, and then channel-hop through the evening until the close-down around midnight. Without physical exercise, Neil tended not to need as much sleep as Toni — but even when they finally turned out the light, it was still Toni's job to wake up hours later and wrestle Neil's body into a different position. The sum total of all this was a state of near collapse, allied to a growing suspicion that she was failing to provide the kind of hourly motivation that Neil needed if he were to start to help himself. "I was just tired all the time and there seemed no end to it. Grange Road was the place we'd been praying for but it just wasn't working. Whatever I did wasn't enough. He just wasn't getting any better. Stoke really was the best place for him".

With the flat to herself and a weekly income of about £45 from Neil's state entitlements, Toni settled down for her own convalescence. At first, Neil had asked her to accompany him to Stoke Mandeville — finding somewhere to live nearby and commuting daily to the hospital. This she declined to do, partly because she needed some time to herself, and partly because — as Eileen immediately pointed out — no one really knew when Neil would be out. It might be a couple of weeks, or a month or two, or even longer. Whatever happened, it was pointless going to the trouble and expense of finding rooms in Aylesbury. Far better she stayed in Petersfield, recharged her batteries, and accompanied Bob and Eileen on the regular visits they planned on forthcoming weekends. With this plan, even Neil finally concurred, asking Keith Wilde to look after Toni in his absence. This, Keith agreed to do. He knew what Toni meant to Neil, and he admired the way she'd stuck by him. As well, he knew she was bored and lonely down at Grange Road and he had a large circle of local friends to whom he could introduce her. As the summer got under way, the pair of them began to go out together.

Back at Stoke, Neil quickly settled into the new routine. Without the cushion of recent injury he had far too much time on his hands and it soon became obvious that the infection was going to be harder to clear up than he'd imagined. Toni's absence had at first made the days seem even longer, but after a while he was obliged to take more notice of his surroundings. "Toni and the folks only came at weekends so I became much more aware of the people around me — nurses, auxiliaries etc — and I learned much more about the running of the place. In a way that was a good thing because the ward was full of much older people — old lags who'd been back time and time again and they taught me an enormous amount about coping with the condition. I see the same thing now when I go round prisons talking to prisoners. It all rubs off. They go in for some minor crime and they come out knowing how to rob a bank. With me in Stoke it was similar. Talking to the blokes in there, I just knew so much more about myself, and the condition, and what was going to happen. In that sense, not having so many visitors was a godsend. Being less protected, I had to work things out for myself."

Bit by bit, Neil began to explore the implications of his tetraplegia, an exercise which offered some surprises. For the first time, he realised how lucky he'd been: one of the recent admissions to the ward had been a woman who'd fallen downstairs and broken her neck. Neil had last seen her a year back at the Intensive Care Unit at Guildford, and she'd had to spend the intervening twelve months at a general hospital because beds at spinal units simply weren't available. The lack of specialist care had resulted in a rash of pressure sores and only now was she given the kind of chance that Neil had long taken for granted.

In Ward Three X he also heard news of some of his buddies from One X, the ward down the corridor in which he'd spent his first five months. Alfonso, for instance, the flamboyant South American who'd been such a comfort during his first weeks, was now living in residential care somewhere in London. Friendless and alone, he'd taken to drowning his high spirits in bouts of heavy drinking and was said to be causing "a serious nuisance and worry". Quite where he'd end up was anybody's guess, though lack of family support lengthened the odds against his ever being able to retrieve any kind of real independence. Dave Perry was another memory of One X, a pale, thin Welshman who'd occupied the bed next to Alfonso and had quickly acquired a reputation as the ward comedian. He'd left Stoke Mandeville for the shelter of his father's flat, but his father had only recently split from his mother and quickly found the demands of his near-helpless son too much to cope with. As a result, Alan, too, had been committed to an institution and was said to be "very depressed". Faced with this news, Neil began to ponder his own situation. Life at Steep had been far from successful but he still had the support of a very close family. Add Toni, and the Grange Road flat, and the prospects were positively rosy.

Toni, by now, was living a life of her own. Through Keith, she'd begun to make other friends locally and she was doing her best to sort out her head before Neil's return. But try as she would, it was impossible to detach Neil from the fact of his tetraplegia. She liked him as a person, loved him even, certainly felt sorry for him, but was frankly intimidated by the long term implications of the relationship. These were too awesome for serious consideration and while Neil was at Stoke Mandeville she postponed all thought of the future. Her present freedoms were too new and too precious to jeopardise in this way and for the time being she was determined to enjoy herself. The obvious partner in this novel enterprise was Keith. "I'd made really good friends with Keith at this point. We used to go out three or four times a week to the Bell or the Green Dragon, and we'd play bar billiards and chat and have a few laughs, all the things I couldn't do with Neil. A lot of people thought it was awful, what we were doing. A lot of people warned me about Keith. They thought it was terrible. Neil's best friend going off with Neil's girlfriend, but the strange thing was it was nothing like that. We really were just friends."

At Stoke Mandeville, meanwhile, Neil's swabs finally told the doctors that the infection in the pressure sore had cleared up. After weeks of careful nursing, Neil was ready for the next step. The management of pressure sores varies from patient to patient, but generally the doctors are faced with two choices. Either the sore can be left to heal of its own accord or the surgeons can decide to operate and close the wound surgically. The former method requires time and a great deal of patience, while surgery usually offers a better chance of an early discharge. In Neil's case, the decision was made to operate. With luck, and good post-operative care, he'd be back at Petersfield in time to enjoy the last of the summer.

The operation itself proved to be an unexpectedly bizarre experience. "There was no point in an anaesthetic, of course, because I couldn't feel anything so they just gave me a Valium and wheeled me off down to the theatre. That was a really strange feeling because you know they've been sticking pins in you and so on to make sure it's going to be OK but here they all are in their green gowns and facemasks and somehow you expect to be put to sleep. The fact that you're not makes the whole thing very dreamlike. You keep thinking they've forgotten or made a mistake or something. I could see what the surgeon was doing in the reflections in various shiny surfaces. That was weird, too. The guy had a little silver chisel and hammer and he was bashing away at the bottom of my spine and I could see all the blood running everywhere and everytime he hit the chisel the vibrations went right through me."

After the last of the infected bone had been chipped away, the surgeon stitched the wound together in layers and Neil was then returned to the ward. One bonus of not having anaesthetic was an immediate cup of tea, plus one of the home made trifles which Eileen was delivering weekly to a small army of appreciative clients on the ward. But Neil's luck, once again, was about to run out. Only weeks after the operation, the top layer of stitches broke and the wound re-opened. This time the doctors abandoned the idea of surgery in favour of more conservative methods: the wound would be taped open and left to heal by itself. This process is called "granulation" and is measured in months rather than weeks. Neil had already been flat on his belly for what seemed like eternity. Ahead of him now stretched another indefinite period of convalescence while his body grew a protective shield over the hole at the base of his spine. The days came and went, bringing with them a growing sense of frustration. "The longer I was there, the more aware I became of that awful contrast between things going on around me the whole time, and nothing ever being achieved. Every day was very busy. And yet, at the end of it, for me, there was nothing to show."

It was during this period that Neil made firm friends around the ward. Fellow patients would wheel across to his bedside and sit chatting for hours on end about themselves and their paralysis and the way their own lives had changed. Neil also became aware of various self-help groups, one of which was the Spinal Injuries Association ('SIA'), a relatively recent venture established in 1974. From literature available at the hospital, Neil learned that the SIA had been set up "to help individuals achieve their own goals, bring about the best medical care and rehabilitation, and stimulate scientific research into paraplegia". These aims were totally in line with Neil's own thinking and he was further heartened by the discovery that the oldest and most vigorous branch of the SIA happened to be in Hampshire. The local branch chairman there was Pat Saunders, himself disabled, who wrote a regular column called 'Pat's Piece' in the Portsmouth daily paper, The News. One of the purposes of this column was to alert people not only

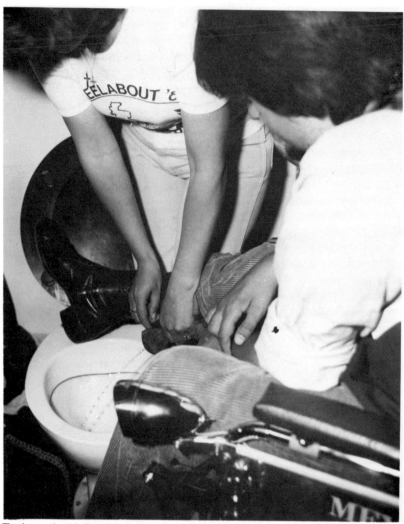

Toni empties Neil's "kipper" leg bag. Neil must drink at least five pints of liquid a day to stay healthy

to the needs of the disabled, but to their rights, and this too seemed to Neil to be a logical step onwards in his own recovery. For too long he'd been the passive recipient of other peoples' favours: medical and otherwise. Soon it would be time to take the initiative himself.

For the time being though, there was the problem of Toni. Hospitalised far longer than he'd expected, Neil felt the relationship increasingly under threat. "Of course I was jealous about Toni. I knew she was free with a place of her own and sometimes she wouldn't appear for two or three weeks and then say she'd had a headache or something and at that point I *knew* something was going on but I never enquired too far because I simply wasn't strong enough to cope with the consequences. It would have broken me. Again, I was absolutely powerless to do anything."

For her part, Toni was beginning to regain her appetite for life. She saw Neil as often as other people's transport permitted, but that was rarely more often than once a week. Because she had nothing more damning on her conscience than evenings at the Green Dragon, she made no secret of the fact that Keith had become a good friend. But Neil was far from convinced. "He suspected Keith from the start, when nothing was actually happening. He used to ask me leading questions at the hospital about how I'd been spending all his money. Sometimes he'd accuse me of keeping Keith on his benefits but I used to shrug it all off. I've never been good with money and he knows it. If I've got it, I spend it, Keith or no Keith."

By this time, late summer, Keith had got to know Toni well. He'd seen her with Neil, and he knew her alone, and the contrast was — understandably — marked. "We had really good times together. When Neil was around she got really wound up, really uptight. But free to do her own thing, she could be really good fun. Obviously we used to talk about Neil a lot. To begin with he was all we had in common. I sometimes thought she might feel trapped by him, by his predicament, but I don't think that was true. She simply thought it was the right — the only — thing to do and if she ever thought seriously about it I guess she assumed it wouldn't last forever. Toni's someone who takes things as they come. It's really that simple."

From Toni's point of view, Keith had become her best friend, but the more she saw of him, the more difficult it was to work out why he never made a pass at her. She understood that Keith was a close friend of Neil, and that Keith might well have qualms about a serious inter-ference in their relationship, but Keith also had a reputation in the town for conquests and she began to take his scruples personally. She'd never before had trouble attracting men and Keith was fast acquiring the status of a challenge. Neil, after all, was ninety miles away and she saw no point in restricting her own freedoms. She'd looked after him for nearly a year and life now owed her some of the simpler pleasures.

The outcome of all this was a drunken interlude at a friend's house in

Petersfield, after which Keith awoke with a severe hangover and an appalling attack of conscience. It was indisputable that Toni had taken the initiative and successfully seduced him, but the blame was equally his for letting events take their course. Later that day he went round to Grange Road to mumble a stricken apology but the exchange became confused again and by the end of the week the affair had become the talk of the town. Some blamed Keith, others Toni. A few, more thoughtful, pointed out that tetraplegia was an experience mercifully remote from most peoples' lives and perhaps the best reaction to Toni's indulgence was a discreet — even sympathetic — silence. Either way, the important point of the triangle was Neil.

Neil was discharged from Stoke Mandeville on the 19th October 1978. Nearly winter again, he travelled slowly back to Petersfield where Toni had done her best to prepare a welcome. But the flat was unavoidably cold, the atmosphere dead, and Neil himself was far from happy. His last weeks in hospital he'd spent in delicious anticipation of getting back home. Home would mean freedom, chat, friends, visits to the pub. He'd get in touch with the SIA and try and find a role for himself in their activities. But when the time finally came to leave, there were still dressings on the pressure sore and the nurses left him in no doubt what would happen if the sore re-opened. There'd be another ambulance, another bed, another three months in hospital. Determined never to set foot in Stoke Mandeville again, Neil was therefore very cautious. The living room he quickly abandoned for the safety of his bed, and once again Toni was back with the non-stop nursing, and the manual evacs, but Neil's very presence was also testing her in other ways. "He came back from hospital that second time expecting a relationship that simply wasn't there. It sounds awful to say so, but I almost didn't notice him. He was almost there on sufferance. I just wanted to be with Keith. I couldn't see very much of him, of course, because I was so busy with Neil, but all I really wanted was out. I'd tasted freedom and that was that."

Eileen at this point was an almost constant visitor, and she began to fear the worst. "I knew there was something blowing up. Toni used to talk to me. It was very hard for her. There was no hoist. No heating. And she'd refused a home help so she was literally on her own. She was really at the end of her tether."

Worried about the possible consequences of a break up, but knowing nothing about Keith, Eileen got in touch with Liz Hardley, the Occupational Therapist. She described Neil as "very depressed" and said that the whole situation was having its effect on Toni. By this time the welfare wheels had begun to grind. The work on the bathroom, and on new access from the garden to the living room, had been started and there were now firmer plans to install central heating. But the latter had been held up by a wrangle about which arm of the bureaucracy should bear the cost — the Social Services at Winchester or the Housing Department at Petersfield — and for the time being Toni and Neil were having to get by with a calor gas heater on loan from the Social Services. Apart from the heating and the access there was also the question of a hoist for transferring Neil's fourteen and a half stone in and out of bed. Liz Hardley, ever willing to help, had turned up with a series of devices but they'd either been too small or too badly designed to cope. In all, the effect on Toni was traumatic. "It wasn't Neil that I disliked but the situation. I was confused about Keith, tired out of my brain, and just not strong enough to cope any more."

Neil, looking back, has nothing but sympathy for Toni but at the time he had too many problems of his own to notice her increasing desperation. "For starters it was literally impossible for me to move around the house. All the fight had been knocked out of me by the extra time in bed. All the physical advances that I'd made that first time in Stoke Mandeville had completely gone. So most days I just stayed in bed, mostly because the pressure sore used to get very red and dangerous, but also because I'd become completely apathetic. The TV was there and everything and it just seemed the safest place to be. The rest of the flat was a farce. The kitchen wasn't really up together and the adaptations were very basic. A couple of door handles had been changed and they were doing the outside door into the living room, knocking a hole in the wall, but they took forever to do it and there was a period of days when we just had plastic sheeting between us and the elements. The whole thing was a joke."

By this time, it was mid-December. For the last couple of years Toni had made it a rule to spend three or four days before Christmas with her mother in London. Her father had departed when Toni was still a baby and the relationship with her mother had become difficult when Toni, barely a teenager, began to run away to live with friends. By the time she met Neil, though, mother and daughter were back on good terms, and the pre-Christmas get-together at the tiny house in Abbey Wood had become a regular event. 1978 was to be no exception, and half way through December, Toni announced that she'd soon be packing for London. Arrangements were made for Neil to be transferred back to Steep where Eileen and Bob would look after him, and Toni promised to return there for Christmas. Of Keith, for obvious reasons, there was no mention. His relationship with Toni had taken second place to Neil's needs and he had little idea of where events might lead next. Neil remained a good friend, though Keith now found their encounters a little strained.

Toni went to London and stayed with her mother for the usual three days. Then she phoned Keith. There'd been a loose arrangement that they might be able to meet in London, and she now suggested that he come up and see her. Keith took a train to Waterloo and they met. That night they booked into the Grosvenor House Hotel under the name of Pipington, using money that Toni had managed to save up. The next day they returned to Waterloo and bought tickets for Petersfield. Before the night at the Grosvenor House Hotel, Toni had intended to accept her responsibilities for Neil and join him at Steep for Christmas, but her fondness for Keith had now reached the point where she knew there was only one decision to make. She told Keith she thought they should leave Petersfield and go away together. Keith agreed. "I think both Keith and I were very aware of the impending scandal, of what people would say, and it took a lot of courage for Keith to do it. He had to come back. It was his home. I could live anywhere".

The station before Petersfield is Liss. At Liss they both got out and hired a taxi to Grange Road where Toni used her front door key to get into the flat and remove her remaining clothes. She felt, she says, "like a burglar". There was medical gear everywhere. The place smelt of Neil. Desperate not to be seen, she and Keith got back in the taxi and then went to a friend's house, partly because they needed time and a telephone to find jobs elsewhere, and partly because there was nowhere else to go. What little money Toni had saved was now gone.

Toni and Keith stayed at Petersfield for two or three days while Keith hunted for work. By this time Neil knew that Toni wasn't coming back. She'd first broken the news on the telephone and in letters routed via London she now did her best to explain why. She talked of feeling "washed out", of her own sense of "failure", and begged Neil not to give up. "Do your best..." she wrote, "... because you've got the strength of mind and body to do it. I know I've disappointed you but now you must show you're made of better stuff than I am. Make a go of things. Don't be frightened of the world. It doesn't bite."

Neil was devastated. Toni had meant everything to him. She'd been his nurse, his physio, housekeeper, cook, lover. Far more than that, she'd been his friend. She'd sat with him, suffered with him, read to him, held his hand. In a world that wanted to put cripples away, she

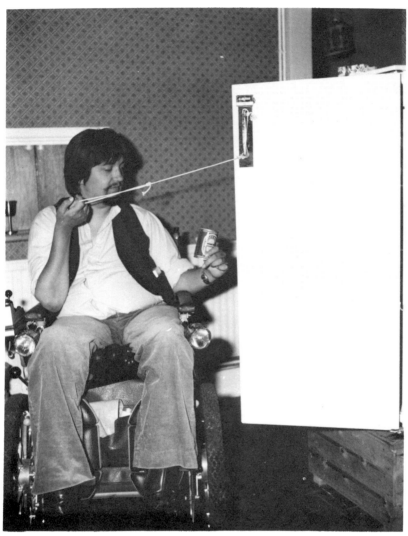

Neil examines part of his daily fluid intake

was his one chance of independence. But now she was gone, and his physical chances of winning her back were a joke. "She phoned and said it was all over, I just couldn't believe it. It hadn't crossed my mind she was leaving for good because I just hadn't thought about it. I was so wrapped up in my own problems that I didn't see things from her point of view. She was my lifeline, and everything else I just took for granted. It never occurred to me that *she* might be depressed and worn out. Strange, that. I see a lot of it now in my own counselling work, with both the disabled and the able-bodied. One partner simply not aware of what's happening to the other. So when Toni said she was going off to see her mum again, I just said yes. Finding out she wasn't coming back was the end of everything."

To Eileen, Neil said very little but she knew him far too well not to guess what was happening inside. "He just gave up. He just stayed in bed and gave up. He wouldn't tell me why, but I think we all knew". At this point a visitor appeared: Keith Wilde. For obvious reasons, Keith had been reluctant to come and see Neil but Toni had insisted. "It was me who got Keith to go and see Neil, chiefly because I wanted Keith to be in the clear with Neil. Neil knew by now that I'd left him and I didn't want him to associate that in any way with Keith. If Keith actually went to see him, the last thing Neil would think was that I was a mile or so away, down in Petersfield."

Keith duly sat at Neil's bedside and the pair of them discussed Toni's absence. Keith said he'd been in touch with Toni by phone, confirmed that she wasn't coming back, but urged Neil to make the best of it. By this time, Keith had secured the promise of holiday work at Pontin's Holiday Camp near Torquay and he and Toni were on the point of leaving. Down in Petersfield, Toni was once again packing her bags. "It sounds awful what we did to Neil that time but it really was for the best of intentions. Of course I felt sorry for him, but I had a life to lead too. I suppose in a way I wanted to find out how he was, to make sure he wasn't doing anything *really* silly."

The next day Toni and Keith set off for Torquay. At the holiday camp they waited on table and served behind the bar. Christmas at Steep came and went. Looking back, Eileen describes it as "glum". On Neil's suggestion, she finally phoned Toni's mother who was aware that Toni had gone to Torquay but knew nothing about her travelling companion. The two women talked for a while, sharing their impressions of what had happened. "We both agreed that Toni felt that Neil had given up and that she was having to do everything. So I started on my campaign to get him to do more for himself in order to get her back. At first he didn't take much notice — it was me just being a busybody again — but then it began to dawn on him and he made a great effort. I used to tell him "You've just made a prop of her, and she's a person with her own needs, and everything you've done to her has just made it harder for her." I knew exactly what he'd done to her because he'd done exactly the same to me. But it was different with me because he was my son. I made allowances. Toni — in the end — didn't."

Down at Torquay, the holiday job came to an end and Toni and Keith were paid off. With the money they'd earned they found a winter let and began to look round for more work, a task which Toni assumed would be easy. "At that point I'd no intentions at all of going back to Petersfield. We were both having such a good time. In fact we never had a bad time. But then we started having hassles finding another job, and not being able to get dole money, and pretty soon we were spent up, and the one thing I didn't want was for the whole relationship to go sour because of money. I just got a feeling that might happen, that we might never make it, simply because we were too expensive."

Throughout this period, Toni had been in touch with Neil, phoning him at regular intervals, reversing the charges, and talking for hours. On the phone, Neil carefully avoided asking her to come back, partly because he didn't want her to say "No", and partly because the important thing was to convince her that he'd changed his ways. In reality, he had indeed changed. Gone were the days in bed, the peremptory orders, the sudden tongue lashings, the abrupt loss of temper. Now he got up every day, fed himself, laid plans for the future. There was talk of a job at the local radio station, and work to do at the local SIA branch. He'd ceased to wallow in his own problems. Now he wanted to take up the cudgels on behalf of others. He'd become, in Eileen's phrase, "a fighter".

On the phone and by letter, Toni did her best to encourage this transformation. She talked of his natural ability, his intelligence, his knack of making friends easily, his determination, and she begged him to make the most of these assets. But always, in the back of her mind, there was the suspicion that it might be a fantasy, a ploy to get her back. Finally, during the course of a particularly long call, she threw him an abrupt challenge. "I gave him an ultimatum. It had to be something bloody hard, something that would prove that he'd got out of bed and got himself together. I said if he really wanted me back he'd have to write me a four-page letter. Any cheating, and he'd blow it. Every word had to be his."

Neil accepted the challenge. "I started the letter the next day. It was the first writing I'd tried since the accident. It took forever, three days and nights. I can't remember exactly what it said but I know that I was missing her a lot and that I thought my life would change and that I was proving it up at Eileen's. The business of actually writing the letter was the major turning point in my life at that stage. Definitely. I used to have a felt tip pen wedged between my index finger and middle finger and thumb with elastic bands round it, and I'd be working so long at the letter that I'd lose what little sensation I had left in my index finger. Eileen would fuss a lot but I'd refuse to have the elastic bands off at all while I was writing and when they finally came off it would be agony and there'd be great gouges out of the fingers and thumb where I'd been struggling away with this damn thing. It was also a great way of getting rid of the frustrations that had been building up. I'd not been able to do anything and so the sheer act of writing the letter did me all the good in the world. The fact that the letter was hard to read at the beginning but completely legible at the end was an achievement. Before Toni went I'd never have got that far. If I'd even started a letter, I'd have got no further than the first paragraph, then thrown it aside. Yes, no question, that was a major change."

The letter went to Toni's mother, and thence to Torquay. Reading it, Toni realised she had no choice. Towards the end of January, Keith went shopping at a local supermarket, leaving Toni at the holiday flat. When he got back he found a note on the table. It was simple and fond and said goodbye. Of Toni's few possessions there was no trace. "I read the note a couple of times and kicked the furniture for a while and then went out and got smashed. Then I sobered up and felt sorry for her. Then I felt sorry for me. Then Neil. It was pathetic. Next day I sent her a telegram telling her she'd done the best thing and wishing her all the luck in the world. Funny thing is, I really meant it".

Toni hitched back to Petersfield, arriving there in the early evening and phoning Neil from a callbox in the Square. She suggested a drink and Bob drove Neil down to Petersfield in the family car. They met in the rain outside the call box. Neil remembers feeling slightly dazed. "I think we went to the Market Inn. I know I felt extreme anxiety, extreme relief, and about twenty thousand other things. I was amazed she'd come back. Afterwards we went back up to Steep and Eileen and Bob sort of disappeared to bed but Toni stayed with me and that was a nice warm feeling, very hard to describe, a feeling of wholeness again. I knew that there was lots of talking to do but just having her back was the best proof that things had really changed."

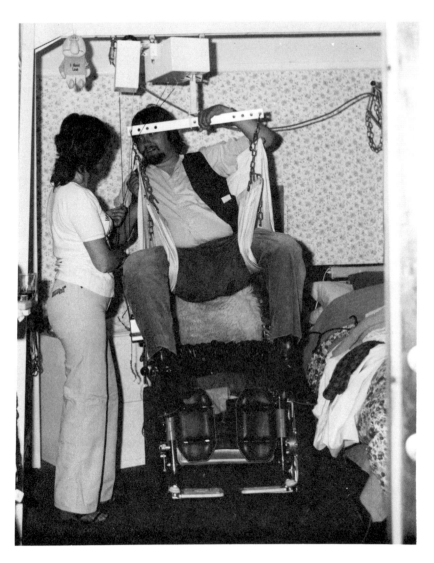

The Radcliffe Hoist in action — Toni helps Neil into bed. See page 96

Chapter Seven

Toni and Neil moved back into Grange Road in the middle of January 1979. At no point during Toni's absence had Neil considered abandoning his hard-won council flat. Indeed, he'd been making plans with a friend who'd look after him but the fact that Toni had returned was the best possible solution. Hours of talking had established the basis for a new relationship, and on this Neil was determined to build.

Toni would henceforth be a real partner, someone different, co-equal, with a life of her own to lead. They'd live together, sleep together, share everything, but from time to time Toni would need a few days to herself. This, Neil would have to accept on trust but never again would she leave him without first explaining why. In this sense — and many others — the initiative had passed almost entirely to Toni, and although this was a reversal of every other relationship he'd ever had, there was simply no choice. Of Keith, there was no mention. Until the writing of this book, Neil hasn't known the details of Toni's month away.

Toni, much to her surprise, found that she was glad to be back. For one thing, the flat looked different. "I'd only been away a month or something but it was totally unrecognisable, like being in a strange house. Eileen had been at it. She'd painted and decorated and put a different carpet in. It didn't look better or worse, just different, almost as though I'd never been there."

By themselves at Grange Road, Neil and Toni now made a new start. All too aware of the consequences of the old regime, Toni tore up the hospital rule book and began to organise Neil's care in a way which took her own sanity into account.

Her first concern was bowel evacuation. Stoke had recommended evacs every two days and had suggested the use of laxatives. This tended to make an unpleasant routine even worse, and Toni had a shrewd suspicion it was unnecessary. "We didn't even discuss it. I just poured all this orange gunk down the sink and bought tons of fresh vegetables instead. Neil hated that, I could tell. He's always thought the green stuff belongs to rabbits. He's a meat and spuds man. But he just kept quiet about it and did what he was told. It cost a fortune but it did the trick. He got much healthier and I managed to cut the evacs down to once every three days until they were a fine art. First I'd give him a suppository then we'd wait fifteen minutes. That's exactly the time it took to drink a cup of tea. Then I'd put him up onto one elbow and help it out with one hand while tapping on his belly with the other. I had these special seamless polythene gloves. It took no time at all. Dead simple. Then I'd get him to push. I'd yell "push" at him and I don't think he could but it made him believe he could and that was what mattered."

Encouraged by this major triumph, Toni turned her attention to other hurdles in the nursing day. One of the cardinal rules of tetraplegic care is a regular change in the body's position to counter the menace of pressure sores. Spinally injured people in wheelchairs are supposed to lift themselves or to be lifted and moved every fifteen minutes; while in bed their bodies must be lifted and turned every three hours. At first Toni had obeyed these rules, but Neil's fourteen stone and her own lack of sleep soon began to tell. The answer, once again, was simply a question of experiment. "As far as the wheelchair was concerned I was just knackered. Four times an hour I was supposed to lift him up, count to twenty and then let go again. That's no joke with someone like Neil so we looked round for different kinds of cushions for his chair. Eventually we found an American design called a Roho. It's made of special rubber and it looks like an open egg box and it cost a fortune (at 1981 prices, £130), but it was worth every penny. With that, and a bit of leverage from his own arms, we had no problems. The bed was easy, too. We were already sleeping in a double bed, which was strictly against the rules, and one night I simply didn't wake up when I should have done so he just didn't get turned. Next day I had a good look for pressure sores but found nothing so we did it again the following night and again there was no damage. Later on we got a special 'ripple' mattress made of tiny inflatable air cells to be on the safe side, but there's never been a problem".

By this time, regardless of how he felt, Neil was forcing himself to get up every day, determined to lead as normal a life as possible — and this, too, made all the difference to Toni. "Most disabled people keep invalid hours. They're up at nine and back in bed by six. But we got up at ten and never went to bed until one or two in the morning, and it made all the difference. For one thing his skin got really tough, and for another it began to change Neil. His whole attitude changed. The hospital rules make you feel like a cripple. I know they're not really rules but only advice and they're supposed to protect you and everything, but you just become a taker. You give in. You stop trying to be independent. But Neil was great. He'd had enough of being sorry for himself and he became incredibly helpful."

Another turning point was the question of drink. "He was supposed to drink five pints of liquid a day to avoid bladder infections, but who wants to drink five pints of water or orange juice? So at the first sign of a headache (one symptom of a bladder infection) I'd drag him off down the pub and we'd have two or three pints which usually put him right. The act of drinking was difficult to begin with. According to the book I was supposed to feed him little sips but there was no way I was going to do that because it made us both look daft so he just had to learn to do it himself. As long as you use a mug with a handle, it's not that hard. And it works. Now, if you look in his fridge, it's full of beer. What they were trying to prohibit at the hospital just happened to be most of the pleasurable things in life and I just wasn't having it."

Grateful for Toni's care and aware that life was getting better by the day, Neil even succumbed to Toni's sartorial tastes. "I used to call him my little rag doll. I could dress him exactly the way I wanted to. I threw out all his baggy trousers and baggy shirts that let his belly hang out and I made him dress in tight gear... really trendy. He looked great."

Throughout this period, Neil and his family had been under close observation from the various care agencies in the area. Everyone agreed that a secure relationship offered Neil the best chance of some kind of future, and Toni's departure therefore caused some concern. The fact that she'd come back and that the pair of them seemed happy, was felt to be a major step forward.

Neil's primary link with the social services had so far been Liz Hardley, the young Occupational Therapist from Alton. Disabled people live on the margins of the welfare state, entitled to a confusion of benefits, pensions, mobility aids, and other forms of mechanical assistance, and it was Liz Hardley's job to match a particular set of needs to the sum total of what was available. Both Neil and Toni were certainly aware that people like Liz were on their side, and they were duly grateful, but sometimes the state's aids were far from practical. As Toni discovered, good intentions simply weren't enough. "There was the saga of the chairs. We got three in all, all supplied by the DHSS.

Neil with live-in friend, Pasha

The first one was a shower/commode chair, all done in non-rusting metal. It had a hole under his backside which meant that I could wash Neil from the underside. That was all fine, but when I tried to get him off it, it was hopeless. The technique was to put one hand under each cheek. the first hand was OK, but the second had got trapped between his backside and the hole, with his body weight bending back my fingers and nearly breaking them. So there was no way I could get him off this chair. Finally I parked it up alongside the bed, put his legs full length on the bed, pushed his body sideways, then ran round the bed to catch him. Very dangerous but it worked. The second chair was a patent device, an indoor electric wheelchair. It was built like a tank and had three wheels, two at the back and one at the front. The problem here was that whenever Neil leaned forward, the chair tipped over. Then the last chair was a special office chair, velvet armrests, swivel mount, with a special control which also swivelled. This was supposed to give tetras full control but the design meant that it swivelled in two directions and because Neil had no control over his bottom half, it was useless."

Incidents like these, though, were mercifully rare. Item by item the flat at Grange Road was being transformed to answer Neil's needs, and although progress was often slow, local officials were doing their best to work through Liz Hardley's original list of adaptations. These had been costed by the council at £1961 but work had been held up while David Hooper, the local Housing Officer, tried to sort out the continuing wrangle of who should pay for the central heating. Neil's consultant at Stoke Mandeville had confirmed that this was important but the Social Services Department at Winchester were reluctant to foot the bill of £650 and so the decision had been returned to East Hants District Council. By the time Neil and Toni moved back into Grange Road in January 1979 there was snow on the ground and the flat was freezing, yet the interminable council memos still passed to and fro until the 19th January when David Hooper was able to contact Neil and tell him that District Council funding for the central heating was "nearly definite".

For Neil, this was excellent news. "By that time we'd really started getting the flat together. There was a bed in the spare room and we were making the living room look decent. We bought a decent music system on HP and we had a settee and chairs and tables and Dad gave us lots of help with the decorating. He also made some working surfaces for the kitchen, and we got a fridge and stuff and the whole place started to come together as a real household. We started to live like normal people, two people, not just a helper and a chair, and we were talking a lot, as well. The whole relationship changed. We started to make decisions together. We took up offers of help from other people which meant that someone else could push the chair when we went out so that Toni could walk beside me instead of behind me and we could actually talk *and* look at each other. We also got a Home Help,

Joanne. She'd come in twice a week to give us a hand with the washing and the cleaning and bits and pieces like that — the things that Toni had no time for. To get the central heating in on top of all that was marvellous news."

Life at Grange Road was undoubtedly getting better, but there were still moments when Neil and Toni became suddenly aware of the permanently thin line which separates the tetraplegic from disaster. One afternoon, Toni went shopping. "It was very unusual for me to leave Neil by himself but on this occasion I had no choice. The heating wasn't in at that point so we had an open fire in the living room. I made him as comfortable as I could in front of the fire but he only had an ordinary hand-propelled wheelchair and he simply hadn't got the strength in his arms to move it. Also the carpet was a reject of Eileen's, full of bumps with the edges turned over, a bit like an assault course. Anyway, I made him comfortable, then went out. Soon afterwards, a burning log fell out of the fire and rolled onto the carpet at his feet and, of course, there was nothing he could do about it. He couldn't even wheel back towards the wall. All he could do was sit and watch the carpet catch fire. Fortunately, someone happened to call round in time and put the fire out, but it really gave me a turn. He'd have been totally helpless. He couldn't even call out properly. His lungs weren't strong enough."

Throughout this period, January to February 1979, Liz Hardley was supplemented by a student social worker. He, too, did his best to act as a middle man between Neil and the various state agencies and in these early months he recorded a catalogue of difficulties and complaints, minor in themselves, but adding up to a feeling of profound frustration. Progress on the central heating seemed once again to have come to a full stop. Council promises had now been confirmed but there was still no date for installation. This meant that Neil was still at serious risk from bronchial infection, especially after Toni's sessions with him in the bathroom. Wet all over, she had to transfer him into the relative warmth of the bedroom before she could begin to dry him. Neil, of course, could only feel the cold above his chest but the rest of his body still cooled faster than was safe and bronchial infections had nasty implications for tetraplegics.

Other worries seemed trivial by comparison but still niggled. There was now a new back door from the living room into the garden, giving wheelchair access round the side of the house to the street, but the door had already warped and was very difficult to open. Inside the house, most of the door handles were still round, making it very difficult for Neil to open or close doors by himself, a lethal handicap in the event of fire. The telephone had been installed with a short lead, mooring it permanently in the hall, and there was still no news on the possible installation of an electric typewriter. The latter would be a vital tool if Neil was to pursue his newly awakened interest in his fellow disabled. He and Toni were also planning to write a joint book on female disability, with another to follow on the everyday problems of the disabled. These projects, plus the possibility of freelance work for the local radio station (Radio Victory) would be an important part of Neil's rehabilitation — and the social worker did his best to sort out the system in Neil's favour.

As well as practical help, the social worker also offered more intimate support and over these first few months of re-adjustment he became a catalyst in the development of a new relationship. In counselling sessions with Neil and Toni he encouraged both of them to express their needs and inhibitions, trying to level the ground between them and thus help chart a path forward. Neil had already done a great deal of thinking along these lines, but the counselling sessions gave him a chance to examine his conclusions afresh.

The key to it all, felt Neil, was the difference in background between himself and Toni. He'd come from a very close family. He'd been used to love and attention and constant physical contact, and though the accident had deprived most of his body of this simplest of pleasures, the rest of him needed to be touched all the more. His shoulders, his neck and his head were supersensitive, the most exposed parts of him, and the closest he could get to someone else was the feeling of their flesh on his. For Toni, this kind of intimacy was a mystery. From birth, her life had been a gradual shedding of every important relationship. Her father she'd never known; her mother she'd moved away from; and her husband she'd regarded as a monster. From then on her life had gone from bad to worse, and it was only the briefest of interludes with Neil, immediately prior to the accident, that had given her any kind of indication that people could be trusted. The result was twofold: on the one hand she had a profound suspicion of touch, sympathy, of any of the overt signs of affection; while on the other she liked Neil, admired him, and felt for him a great deal of compassion. But compassion was no substitute for what Neil wanted and when she began to sort her feelings out she suspected that she simply wasn't capable of meeting his needs. Neil wanted love, but love — his sort of love — wasn't there to be had.

One step away, though, was a mutually satisfying sex life, and in this respect things were definitely getting better. "To begin with I was trying to please him which was obviously impossible because he couldn't come. So he started figuring out ways of pleasing me. He got really good with his mouth. It was quite hard for me to begin with to get rid of all my inhibitions but after a while it was fine."

As winter gave way to spring, life at Grange Road began to settle down. Friends became newly important. Faces from the old days began to reappear and the living room was seldom empty. Toni sometimes felt that this influx of empty stomachs had its drawbacks. Money was sometimes tight and she occasionally felt that food, smokes, and even the odd loan were taken for granted, but Neil thrived on the company. "It was great. I met people like Mark Lawson again, an old friend from the guitar days, and he'd come round and pick out some favourite tunes on his guitar. Things like Donovan's Tangerine Puppet. He'd often stay and he used to eat with us a lot and that used to nark Toni somewhat but people like him were a real help because it meant that Toni could get away from time to time and they'd look after me, dump me in bed after we'd had a few drinks down the pub. That was great because these friends had stopped thinking of me as a cripple and started thinking of me as a human being again."

Apart from casual calls from friends, Toni and Neil also acquired a series of lodgers, partly to help out with the rent, and partly to provide a back-stop in case Toni couldn't cope. The first of these was a friend called John. He was an immense help to Neil and Toni but his taste for ale finally led to yet another crisis.

During the day, Neil was generally confined to a wheelchair but the chair was too upright for Neil's comfort and John often lifted him into the relative luxury of one of the fireside armchairs. This manoeuvre required exceptional strength and was totally beyond Toni. One evening in March, John lifted Neil into his favourite armchair and left for the pub, promising to return in time to transfer Neil back into his wheelchair prior to bed. Hours passed. Then the phone rang with the news that John was far too drunk to drive home and would be spending the night at a friend's flat. With Neil still anchored to the armchair it was therefore up to Toni to get him back into the wheelchair.

For an hour she tugged and pulled, trying somehow to lever Neil's bulk forward onto his feet while Neil did his best to summon some helpful spasm of movement, but nothing seemed to work. At one point they seriously considered phoning the police for another pair of hands. Finally, though, Toni somehow managed to haul Neil out of the chair and wrestle him into bed. At the time, the effort left her too exhausted to notice any specific pain but next day she awoke to find herself unable to move. The doctor was called and diagnosed a slipped disc in her lower back, the direct result of the previous evening's labours. Bob arrived with a board to slip under the mattress, and the next month she spent flat on her back while friends and relatives took care of Neil. Toni's back is now permanently weakened, but one by-product of the incident was the swift arrival of a Radcliffe Hoist. Toni and Neil had been pressing for this device for months. Comprising a beam, with two supports at either end, it straddled the bed and enabled Neil to be strapped into a canvas support, hoisted from his chair, moved laterally along the line of the beam, and then lowered onto the bed. The lifting and transferring were taken care of by a pair of electric motors, thus leaving Neil's helper with the relatively simple task of fitting the canvas support. For Toni, it was a major advance on the now risky business of manual transfers.

Another lodger, who replaced John, was Jan Heidecker, the school-friend of Neil's referred to in Chapter One. Now 19, she first used Grange Road as a bolt hole in the dying days of a particularly traumatic affair, but when Toni invited her to move in she gladly accepted, and over the next few months she and Toni became close friends. Jan was astonished at how much sheer physical labour was involved in Neil's care, and she understood only too well how Toni still needed the odd evening off. On many of these occasions the two of them would go out together, but other nights she'd stay and look after Neil. For Neil, these evenings were a challenge. Jan was young and attractive. The house was empty. But, try as she might, Jan found it very difficult to accept Neil's bluff dismissal of his own paralysis. "One of the problems with Neil was trying to cope with his ego. He never thought twice about being handicapped and he didn't expect you to and that occasionally led to awkward situations. The last thing I ever wanted him to think was that I thought he was some kind of freak."

For her part, Toni was well aware of Neil's roving eye. By now she knew herself well enough to accept that her long term future with Neil was non-existent. It wasn't something that she ever told him but her life now revolved around the slow, painstaking process of making him as independent as possible so that one day he might be able to fend for himself. The intercession of another female — someone whom Neil might fall in love with, and who might be able to respond in kind — would be a welcome short cut, but it was nothing she took for granted.

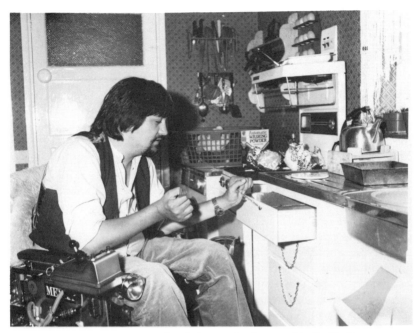

Neil hunts for cutlery — note the chains on the drawers (Toni's idea!)

For the time being their life together worked well enough, and for that she was duly grateful. "For the most part he was a changed man, he really was. He was thoughtful. He was starting to help himself. And more than that he was starting to help others, especially me. He really looked after me. There'd be clothes and flowers and trips down the pub. Anything I wanted, I could have. He was turning into a man again. It was lovely."

As the months went by, Toni and Neil took more frequent trips out. Like most towns, Petersfield wasn't built for wheelchairs but Neil's enthusiasm for real life made all the difference. The usual obstacles were no less difficult but Neil simply responded afresh to the challenge of a high kerb-stone, or a narrow doorway, building up a mental index which would later serve him well. The Post Office, for instance, was impenetrable because of its steps. The bank likewise was out of the question. Telephone boxes were impossible. Supermarket check outs, a nightmare. Everywhere they went, Neil and Toni found fresh evidence that serious disability involved not one but two penalties: one physical and the other social. The doctors had done their best with the first but the second lay in the hands of a society which generally preferred to look the other way.

Ever ambitious, Toni one day proposed a meal out, suggesting a restaurant in the town centre. "It was the first time we'd been out like that so I'd planned everything to make it as good as possible for Neil. I'd made sure the doorway was wide enough and the step wasn't too high and I'd gone right through the menu looking for the easiest food to chop up so that Neil wouldn't make a mess. Kebabs sounded OK because they were in lumps already so I ordered those. For some reason I'd assumed kebabs came with chips, but of course, they came with rice, and that was impossible. The rice went everywhere, all over this nice red carpet, and the manager's face was a picture. He said it was OK because I suppose he had to, but you could tell he was livid. People in wheelchairs simply had no right to eat in restaurants. They belonged in special homes where they could spill what they liked."

Neil, in particular, became quickly impervious to other people's embarrassment. If anything, the reactions of others in shops or pubs or other public places, became a source of great fascination, an endless case study in the way people couldn't cope with the sight of a wheelchair. "Most people were kind but a lot of the kindness was the wrong sort. They were kind because they felt sorry for me. They saw I was young and they saw I was in a wheelchair and they saw Toni pushing and they felt sorry for her, too. What they didn't realise was that we didn't feel the least bit sorry for ourselves. All we wanted was the bloody door opening."

This acute and growing awareness of his impact on others was fast assuming a real importance in Neil's development. His second spell at Stoke had already shown him what the disabled could do for each other, and through the Spinal Injuries Association he was equally determined to share his growing confidence with his fellow disabled. But now he began to realise how much the able bodied also needed help. Preaching independence for the disabled meant nothing without the active support of the society they'd have to rejoin. "It was after I'd begun standing up for myself that I realised how many others needed standing up for too. After what I'd been through, there's every incentive to write yourself off. People are very kind and everything but what they're actually saying is "Don't worry, you'll be taken care of." But we're not parcels. We're people. We want a life of our own. We don't need protecting. We want the same chance to make mistakes that everyone else gets."

Quite where this new awareness would lead Neil was still far from certain, but looking back, he remembers the whole of this period, 1979 to 1980, with great fondness. With Toni's support he'd proved to himself that life could be challenging, worthwhile, and productive. The gloomy days at Stoke and Dunhill Mews now seemed light years away. He had a relationship he was proud of, a place of his own. He had mobility, a little money, and friends. The important freedoms were his for the taking and in the sense that really mattered, he no longer felt the least bit handicapped.

It was at this point that yet another piece of the jigsaw fell into place. Five miles north of Petersfield there's a Cheshire Home called Le Court. Opened in 1954, it was the first of the Cheshire Homes and provided a working model for the dozens which quickly followed.

The idea, in essence, was simple. The severely disabled would be offered a lifelong home in a secure and kindly environment with all the necessary care facilities. Each home would be independently run as a genuine community and residents' fees would be met — where appropriate — by the relevant local authority. Thus the Cheshire Homes would offer a real alternative to long stay hospitals or the care of well-meaning but hard-pressed relatives. There are now 67 Cheshire Homes in Britain and more than a hundred abroad, but Le Court remains one of the most famous.

Neil first went up to Le Court in 1979. There he met some of the 54 residents for whom the place was home for the rest of their lives. For many it was a source of great security and comfort, but for others it meant an inevitably ghetto-like existence, physically removed from the perils and stimulations of the world outside. For them the answer would have been a home in the community, living side by side with the able bodied, but so far that choice simply wasn't available.

By 1979, though, there was a new feeling in the disabled world, a fever for real independence, and this germ had spread as far as Le Court where a handful of residents had been making active plans to live outside. These residents Neil now met, and conversations at Le Court began to open his eyes to the wider implications of his own struggle.

One of the Le Court residents was Philip Mason, a 38 year-old ex-national gymnastics coach who'd broken his neck during a practice session. His injury was particularly high, C3, and he had no feeling or control below the neck. For him, Le Court had been a godsend but eight years on the margins of society had done nothing to suppress his appetite for real life and he'd devoted a great deal of time to trying to find ways of returning to the community. As it happened, he was

99

shortly to marry one of the Le Court care attendants and set up home with her in nearby Whitehill, but this happy personal solution to the problem was entirely fortuitous and did nothing to shake his belief that every disabled person deserved a genuine choice: either to live within, or without society.

A fellow resident who shared this view was John Evans, a 29 year-old tetraplegic who'd broken his neck in a mountaineering accident in New Mexico. Not wanting to impose himself on his family, he'd also accepted a place at Le Court. For this he too, was genuinely grateful, but he made no secret of his desire to move back into the real world as soon as possible. The problem was, how?

With another resident, Philip Scott, a young motor racing driver who'd broken his neck at the Thruxton Circuit, the two men began lobbying local authorities, grant committees, voluntary organisations, and departmental officials at government level in a bid to fund their ideas. Two years later, their efforts would acquire a title ("Project '81") and some modest success but now — in 1979 — the plan was still gaining shape.

For Neil, aware that Le Court could all too easily have become his own home, concepts like the infant Project '81 were very exciting and he'd return from Le Court to bombard Toni with ways in which he too, might be able to participate in the newly aggressive, rights-conscious mood which was beginning to sweep the world of the disabled. Quite what his role might be, and exactly where it might take him, was still a mystery. Little did he know that the answer was barely twelve months away.

Chapter Eight

Throughout this book, Bedales School crops up time and time again and as far as Neil's accident was concerned, the school was involved from the start. Bob was given compassionate leave to shuttle back and forth between Steep and Stoke Mandeville, and when Neil was eventually due for discharge, it was Bedales' sixth formers who helped Bob built the concrete ramp to the rear entrance to the cottage. Later, when Neil was back at Steep and badly in need of company, that too came from Bedales. In every sense, the school and its staff stood squarely behind Bob in the fight to get Neil back into life, no more so than in the saga of Neil's electric wheelchair.

By 1980, Neil and Toni had been living at Grange Road for nearly two years. In most respects the flat was now adapted for Neil's needs. The warped rear door into the living room had been sorted out and a path built round the side of the house to provide access from the street. Inside, door handles had been changed, book shelves built, the kitchen reorganised, and the bathroom combined with the once-separate lavatory. The bedroom hoist worked perfectly and — most important of all — the central heating had been installed. For £2000 of council money the flat was now warm, safe, and accessible. Neil's only remaining restraint was his wheelchair.

Wheelchairs are supplied free to all disabled people under the National Health Service on the recommendation of a hospital consultant or a GP. There are a number of available models, but most users settle for a Zimmer, or an Everest and Jennings. Both are sturdy and perfectly adequate but lack any kind of power source. Indoor electric wheelchairs are also available under the NHS but the only outdoor models they're prepared to supply have to be operated by someone else (in NHS parlance "an attendant"). For Neil, this would leave him as dependent on other people as if he still had a hand propelled chair and was therefore unacceptable. Whatever the price, he was now determined to become as independent as possible. If the means could be found, he needed an outdoor electric chair.

Electric wheelchairs have been on the market for years. They're sold by a number of manufacturers, but some of the best come from a firm in Leeds called Meyra. Their 322 model was widely recognised to be the Rolls Royce of the wheelchair world, and it was this model on which Neil had set his heart. German designed, but distributed under licence from Leeds, the 322 model draws power from two 12 volt batteries and has a top speed of 6 Kmh. It can travel thirty four miles on a single charge and can cope with fields, sand, snow, and kerbs as high as 7". A year later, in Bournemouth, Neil was to take one up a flight of 13 steps. The only drawback with the Meyra chair is the price. At 1980 prices a chair would cost Neil over a thousand pounds.

The answer to this otherwise insoluble problem came yet again from Bedales. Like many other schools, Bedales is almost constantly raising funds for one cause or another, partly because it's a useful outlet for youthful initiative, and partly because it builds valuable bridges to the world outside. Late in 1979, Bob Slatter had a casual conversation with a colleague at the school, and the colleague inquired whether there was anything important that Neil still required. Bob thought about it for a moment and then mentioned the electric chair. Thus was the appeal begun.

Over the next few months, the Bedales' pupils began to contribute to the fund. They held jumble sales, chopped wood, ran errands for local housewives, and by the end of the year they were well on the way towards the target figure. At this point it was decided to hold a concert in the New Year to top up the appeal. Bedales has a fine musical reputation, and arrangements were made to invite a string quartet from Cambridge — old friends of Bedales — to provide the evening's principal attraction. Tickets were sold around the area and a firm of caterers — Fairfields from Portsmouth — offered to donate a lavish buffet to be consumed during the interval.

The concert at Bedales took place on the 16th March and a delighted Neil found himself on the receiving end of a brand new Meyra chair. Speeches were made, donations acknowledged, and during the course of the buffet meal Neil enquired how best he might repay the gift. Patrick Nobes, the headmaster, thought about Neil's enquiry for a moment and then came up with a suggestion. 1981, he pointed out, had been designated International Year of Disabled People (IYDP). If the chair lived up to Neil's expectations, wouldn't it be worthwhile to tour the country raising money for the provision of similar chairs? The idea caught on at once, and by the end of the evening Neil was convinced it would work.

Over the next few months, the notion of a grand tour acquired a firm shape. While Neil explored the freedoms conferred by his new chair, Patrick Nobes pondered the practicalities of sending a young tetraplegic on a gruelling 2000 mile journey round the British Isles. How much support would he need? Where would the additional transport come from? Where would he and his helpers sleep at night? The answer to the latter question proved simpler than he'd expected. At one of the regular meetings of the Society of Headmasters of Independent Schools, Patrick Nobes inquired whether his fellow headmasters en route would be each prepared to offer one night's accommodation to Neil and his colleagues. With one exception, they all said yes.

At this point, Patrick Nobes handed the detailed planning over to Mike Mills, the school's Assistant Bursar, a small, broad, quietly spoken accountant who already knew Neil well. On the basis of the promised accommodation, he called in Neil and Bob Slatter and began to plot a detailed itinerary. IYDP was still half a year away, but it was already evident that the trip was to be a formidable undertaking.

Neil, meanwhile, was considering the implications of the idea. The kicking off point seemed simple enough. Raise lots of money. Buy lots of wheelchairs. Make lots of cripples happy. In its own terms, that was entirely worthwhile. Already he was aware that the Meyra chair had transformed his own life. Gone were the days of polite dependence on others. Now he could wheel wherever he chose. If he wanted to go to the pub, it was ten minutes away. If he wanted to drop in on friends, it was simply a precautionary phone call to make sure they were in. If he wanted to take Toni shopping, *she* could sit on *his* knee. Petersfield had become his for the taking — and by giving others the means to buy similar chairs, he'd be able to offer the same independence. Fine. But the tour was something else, as well. By definition, he'd be going places, meeting people, spreading the word. Not simply about the marvels of the Meyra chair, but what it was like to be crippled in all four limbs and want to remain a member of the human race, to be able to live fully, usefully, and well. The latter, Neil decided, was the real message. If IYDP was about anything, it was about society's preparedness to make room for people like him, to accept that his desire to live an independent life wasn't impractical or impertinent but entirely natural. His right to life, a civilised life, was as fundamental as anyone else's, lucky enough to be able-bodied. Accept that single premise, and the rest — the high kerb-stones, the awkward access, and all the other subtle forms of discrimination — would follow.

In July 1980, with plans for the trip beginning to take shape, Neil, Toni, Bob and Eileen took a holiday aboard a narrow boat on the Grand Union Canal. Specially designed and built by the Spinal Injuries Association on the proceeds of a highly successful appeal, the boat (called 'Kingfisher') had lifts fore and aft and could be controlled from a wheelchair. As the boat puttered north through an endless series of locks, the family discussed the forthcoming project, turning it over and over in their minds, examining it from every angle. The broad itinerary would take them up the left hand side of the country and down the right. Neil's chair would be fitted with a mileometer and this would provide the key to sponsorship. Companies should be approached for block donations or help in kind, while the media should be chivvied for editorial support. With good luck and thorough planning, there was no reason why they shouldn't aim for a final total of £100,000.

With the holiday at an end, Neil and Toni returned to Grange Road where Jan was still in residence. While they were away, Jan had given the Petersfield gossip machine some fresh titbits by beginning an affair with Keith, and she was far from certain about Toni's reaction. Toni's full time involvement with Keith had come to an end with Toni's return to Neil, but she knew that Toni was still fond of Keith, still saw him from time to time, and that Toni might be correspondingly upset about this latest development. Her fears, though, were groundless. For one thing, Toni had broken her hand on a lock gate and was more than grateful for Jan's help with Neil; and for another, she was detached enough to know that resentment was pointless. "I was the one who originally recommended Keith to Jan. No one thought it would last but it did. There was no point being jealous because that way I'd have lost at least one good friend. As it is, we've all stayed friends."

More than that, Toni was beginning to suspect that Neil was serious about the fund raising tour, and that it might actually happen. If it did and if it acquired the promised scale, then it would surely launch Neil on a career of his own, an involvement which would provide her with the honourable discharge she'd been looking for. After three years, she began to sense an end to it all.

The summer over, the planning began in earnest. A small committee was established and regular monthly meetings were held at Dunhill Mews. At the centre of the committee were the Slatter family (Mum, Dad and the three brothers) plus Mike Mills, but one of the newcomers to the project was a young cub reporter from The News, called David

Glanz. He'd met Neil in connection with a local story about the disabled, a subject in which he had a personal interest, but he'd stayed at Grange Road longer than he'd intended, listening to Neil expounding on his plans for the forthcoming trip. "Neil was very good at spotting people who might be able to help him and I suppose I fell into that category. He knew they needed media coverage and he thought I might be the bloke. I admired him though. Compared to others I'd met, he was aggressively disabled. He'd come out of the closet. He knew what he wanted and he was determined to get it."

David Glanz thought about Neil's suggestion for a couple of days, and then returned to Grange Road. "I had my doubts about the project, chiefly because I don't think it's right for charity to do the Government's job for them. And as a socialist I wasn't too keen on the role of Bedales as a public school. But in the end I said I'd do it, on the condition that it wasn't just a money-raiser, a heart-strings appeal. It had to be a consciousness raiser as well."

With this reaction, Neil was delighted. Not only did Glanz's beliefs tally exactly with his own, but the young journalist was able to give the ideas a more precise shape, a talent he extended to the plans for the forthcoming tour. At the next committee meeting, there was a need to give the project a title. Soon they'd be sending out letters, circulating press releases, bidding for sponsorship. They'd need something bold and eyecatching to head the appeal. Various acronyms were suggested. Someone thought they should describe the tour in factual terms — Hampshire Tetraplegic's Tour of the United Kingdom to Raise Money and Awareness of the Needs of Disabled People — but it lacked a certain punch. Finally David Glanz suggested the phrase 'Wheelabout'. It was crisp, accurate and punchy. It would look good on letterheads. There were murmurs of approval. Someone else suggested adding '81'. There was a vote. It was approved. Henceforth their joint efforts were to be known as 'Wheelabout '81'.

At this point, October 1980, the project was quickly gathering momentum. By now there was a definite itinerary, with confirmed nightly stops at public schools en route. The Wheelabout would begin in Petersfield Square on May 5th 1981. From there it would head west to Winchester, Romsey, Blandford, Wells and Bristol. From Bristol it would cross the Severn Bridge into Wales, head north through Hereford, Shrewsbury, and Oswestry, and thence into Lancashire. From Manchester the route went north again into Scotland, crossing from Glasgow to Edinburgh, then turning south through Newcastle and Yorkshire, back into the East Midlands, through London, and finally home again to Petersfield. On day fifty-four, June 27th, the Wheelabout would formally end at Portsmouth.

In all, the Wheelabout would thus cover a ground mileage of 2000 miles. Most of this would be in a convoy of support vehicles, but outside every town or city en route Neil would be unloaded from his vehicle — hopefully a specially adapted ambulance — and would wheel into the town centre. These excursions would serve two purposes. Firstly they'd begin to notch up the vital wheelchair mileage on which the sponsorship would depend, and secondly they'd give Neil first-hand experience of mobility problems from town to town. Letters had already gone out to every town hall en route, and a formal meeting with the mayor would give Neil the ideal platform for the expression of his views. In this way he could highlight local blackspots, draw attention to particular difficulties, and generally invite the able bodied to share the view from the wheelchair. It was an ambitious plan, but it offered the perfect vehicle for the kind of crusade to which Neil and David Glanz were now committed. "Privately I think Neil doubted whether he'd actually make £100,000 but in a sense that didn't matter because he never cared about the money. It was the consciousness that mattered to him."

With the route established, the pace quickened. Bob Chambers from the Petersfield Lion Clubs wrote to his colleagues round the country in a bid for support and they agreed to provide an escort of fellow disabled to meet Neil on the outskirts of their own towns or cities. The nightly stop-overs had already been fixed, but the WRVS now stepped in with an offer of a midday meal from their local branches up and down the country. Tell us how many, they said, and leave the rest to us.

Another local friend "Jock" Trodden and his girlfriend, Gwyn, joined the project and organised an invaluable communications system based on Storno radios which would assure constant vehicle-to-vehicle contact.

The size of the Wheelabout was by now established. At the heart of the convoy was a ten year old ambulance, donated by the Hants Area Health Authority, and quickly christened 'Gloria'. Specially adapted by Wadham Stringer, a local garage, it was equipped with loading ramps and a set of retaining bolts to secure Neil's chair to the floor inside. A support vehicle, a brand new V.W. van, was supplied by Meyra, the Leeds-based company which had manufactured Neil's chair. Delighted by his sales efforts on their behalf, they'd also donated a small Honda motor bike and a back-up chair. On the road, the crew would generally number six, with changes in personnel at key points en route. Getting people to and from the Wheelabout was obviously going to be costly but this problem was solved by the National Bus Company who offered free travel for any Wheelabout crew members in return for publicity.

While plans were being confirmed for the Wheelabout itself, a quite separate fund raising operation was under way. Special sponsorship forms were drawn up and printed, offering a would-be sponsor a choice of donations — either a fixed sum per mile or a one-off payment regardless of distance achieved. With a covering letter, these forms were then despatched nationwide to business addresses culled from a publication called 'Britain's Top One Thousand Companies'. Many companies didn't bother to reply. Others sent good wishes but little else. Some, though, were more generous, and as the net was cast wider and wider, the money and the promises started to flow in.

The Transport and General Workers Union, to which Bob belonged, promised "total support" and contacted their branches up and down the country for donations and practical aid. Local companies like Tricorn Travel and Condor International sent cheques for £100. The Japanese Mitsubishi Bank donated £85. The Langstone Harbour Fishermens' Association collected £25. An anonymous peer sent a cheque for £100. And Mrs. Vi Oakley, 76, blind and semi-deaf, presented half her weekly pension. These and hundreds of other donations took Wheelabout past the point of no return.

By now it was 1981 and time for a dress rehearsal. The neighbouring town of Midhurst was chosen for a trial run, partly because the distance (14 miles) was ideal, and partly because the Wheelabout crew had been invited to a charity rugby match to be held in late March at the nearby King Edward VII Hospital. A Transit support van was borrowed, and the wheelchair readied for the big test. When the day arrived, though, the weather was appalling and the convoy left Petersfield in driving rain.

Neil led the cavalcade in the Meyra chair, wearing a rainproof cape and broad grin. Behind him came the Transit van and then Bob's Lada car. A police motor cyclist rode escort until the Hampshire/West Sussex border, where he handed over to traffic police from the neighbouring force. At its cruising speed of four miles an hour, the convoy crawled into Midhurst in time for an unplanned lunch at the Egmont Arms, a comfortable pub in the town centre. There, Neil's efforts provoked a spontaneous collection from the Sunday lunchtime drinkers which raised an unexpected £40.

Much encouraged, Wheelabout headed out of the town again for the charity match where the afternoon's good works raised a further £500. That night, back in Petersfield, the Wheelabout team celebrated their success. The wheelchair had performed faultlessly and Neil showed no signs of obvious damage. His efforts had caught the public's imagination and the money came rolling in. At the time, the Midhurst run seemed the best possible omen for the Wheelabout proper, but there were two further consequences which only became apparent later.

The first concerned the attitude of the police. On the busy country road between Petersfield and Midhurst, Neil's convoy had been a quite unexpected hazard for other motorists, and the escorting police had become seriously alarmed about the possibility of an accident. Driving a powered wheelchair on the highway in the absence of footpaths or pavements is perfectly legal, but a lengthy memo was subsequently sent from the Chief Inspector at Petworth to his counterpart at Petersfield. The memo described in detail the events of the previous Sunday, and ended thus: "I have every sympathy with the charitable objectives of this young man, and nothing but admiration for his personal courage, but surely there must be other ways of raising funds. Any unnecessary addition to traffic on our roads is to be deplored. The present proposal is foolish and anti-social, in that it will cause delays and frustrations to other drivers, and create ideal conditions for a serious collision. I cannot believe that the organisers have given proper consideration to all of the issues, and in particular to the possible tragedy that they may be about to construct. I would be pleased if you would do whatever you can to dissuade them."

Conscious that they depended on all kinds of goodwill, including that of the police, the Wheelabout crew duly amended their plans to route Neil onto pavements and footpaths, a policy which assured police co-operation wherever they went.

The other consequence of the Midhurst trip was more productive. Guest of honour at the charity rugby match had been Patrick Moore, the celebrated star-gazer who happened to live locally. He'd been much impressed by meeting Neil and had promised to do whatever he could to arouse television interest within the BBC. For David Glanz, by now the Wheelabout Press Officer, this was a glorious windfall, and within weeks he was beginning to field regular calls from television and radio producers. This publicity had a self-generating effect and by the end of April Neil had become a public figure. Appearances on BBC Nationwide, Southern Television, Radio Victory, Radio Solent, and prominence in the columns of a number of local papers, made him aware for the first time of the real implications of Wheelabout. In the International Year of Disabled People, he'd become the media's favourite cripple.

To onlookers, the transformation in Neil was remarkable. Mike Mills, the Bedales Assistant Bursar, had known Neil for years. "It was impossible not to be moved by the visible effect it was having on Neil. I actually watched him change. He became extremely confident. By this time we were having meetings every fortnight and he'd be in charge. No nonsense. No waffling. Strictly the business in hand. He knew exactly what he wanted. I think to begin with he wasn't at all sure of himself. In fact he was slightly overwhelmed by the support from the school, and in the interest from the media, and all the attention, but it was marvellous the way he got on top of it all. He changed completely. He became very shrewd. Very deft. I don't think he cared about the money. To him, Wheelabout taught him what was possible, in terms of pulling the right political levers, of getting through to people about the real needs of the disabled."

Another onlooker, Toni, saw the same kind of changes but was glad for a different reason. Throughout the planning for the trip, she'd made a conscious effort not to get involved. Where there was work to be done, typing for instance, she'd do it. Night after night she'd sit up with Neil and try and share his enthusiasm. Yet she still kept her distance from the detailed planning, refusing to attend meetings and preferring to avoid the publicity. On one occasion that had proved impossible and a full page feature in the Sunday Times Colour Supplement had described her as "Neil's wife". With that label she took issue, partly because it wasn't true, and partly because she'd now made a firm — if private — decision that Neil would soon be strong enough to permit her to go her own way. "I really made the decision to finally leave Neil at the beginning of 1981. I'd always told myself that I'd go once he was properly independent and I think by that time I'd recognised the Wheelabout as my escape route because Wheelabout would be on-going. No way would it end at the end of the journey. There'd be all kinds of things for him to do. He'd be in great demand. He'd be famous. But I didn't tell him at this point, because I knew that if I did, he'd never do the Wheelabout." For the time being, therefore, Toni continued to give Neil whatever support he needed. She was still his nurse, his best friend, and his lover, and that would remain her function on the Wheelabout itself.

With the grand departure only days away, local interest was now

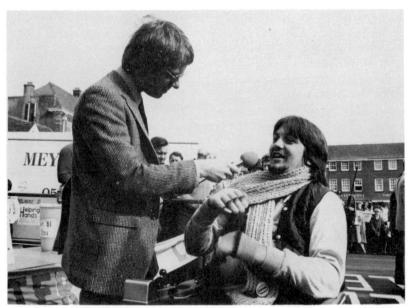

Neil gives the first of many Wheelabout interviews to Rob Widdows of Radio Victory

May 5th, 1981. A final good luck kiss for Neil before the Wheelabout sets off

intense. Whatever it is that infects the British on these occasions had certainly hit Petersfield, and there was a rash of eccentric if well meaning acts of private fund raising. Richard Matthews, a seven year old from Neil's home village of Steep, announced his intention of doing sponsored sit-ups and spent a sweaty Saturday morning thereby raising £30. There were jumble sales, guess-the-weight-of-the-cake competitions, charity darts matches, and a lengthy South Downs hike by a local doctor, also sponsored. A group of local musicians, friends of Neil's had already formed a special band for the occasion — 'Phonads' — and now cut a celebratory disc. Three members of the group — Dave Futcher, 'Tizzy' Stokes and Neil Mercer — were also to become members of the Wheelabout road crew. Finally, word came from the County Council Headquarters in Winchester that the County Council had decided to sponsor Neil themselves at the rate of £2 per mile, a donation which promised a minimum of £2000. By the 4th of May, 'W' day minus one, the fund raising prospects looked extremely rosy.

Neil's departure from Petersfield Square was perfect. There was a band, flags, children. The Vicar said a prayer, the crowds pressed in on Neil, the TV cameras churned, and Toni offered the morning's hero a good luck peck on the cheek. As the church bell tolled ten o'clock Neil made a brief speech, accepted the first of hundreds of cheques, and lifted an arm in farewell. Then the wheelchair jolted into motion and the Wheelabout was off. Behind him, the crowd cheered and then began to disperse. Some people said he was mad, others felt sorry for him, but no one disputed his courage. For someone who'd spent half his recent life in bed, he'd already come a very long way.

Once on the road, the Wheelabout quickly settled into a routine. Each day's schedule revolved around a series of carefully pre-arranged meetings with mayors, transport chiefs, architects, local disabled groups and other assorted dignitaries. The distances between towns had been carefully measured and the mileage translated into journey times. Thus, in theory, each day should yield its treasure of consultations, publicity and windfall cheques.

In practice, of course, things went wrong. The schedule was far too tight for comfort and barely left room for map-reading mistakes, bad weather and all the other pitfalls of long distance travel. In addition, Neil was rapidly becoming famous and as the word spread ahead of the Wheelabout, more and more organisations phoned Wheelabout headquarters at Bedales wanting to arrange last minute detours from the route. Wherever possible, these requests were fulfilled but for Bob in particular, the result was an almost permanent state of anxiety. As he kept explaining to the latest batch of mayors, aldermen and local civic worthies peering bemusedly into the middle distance, Wheelabout was nearly always late.

Nevertheless, the mileage began to mount on the Meyra chair and as the days went by Neil slipped easily into his new role. In a sense he had everything on his side. He was doing the right thing for the right reason in the right year, and yet the speed with which he acquired the key skills was very impressive. The meetings with the Mayors for instance, had all the makings of a public relations disaster. Because wheelchair access to Town Halls was often impossible, the meetings often happened on the street. The Mayor would be wearing his chain of office. His wife would be wearing her best dress. Cameras would be present. Reporters would be scribbling notes. A crowd would gather. Nothing could be less calculated to promote the fruitful exchange of information about the problems of the disabled. Yet it was Neil who had the lightest touch, who defused the situation with a joke or a smile, who gently took the town's elders to task for high kerb stones, or inaccessible shops, or any of the other half dozen cripple traps he'd noticed on the journeys in. The Mayors were at first amazed by this, and then impressed, and then touched or perhaps saddened, and found themselves agreeing, and promising to get things done, and even — in some cases — meaning it. At the end of each encounter — normally no longer than ten or fifteen minutes — Bob Slatter would produce the Wheelabout scroll, a length of parchment specially designed by the Head of the Bedales Art Department and the Mayor would be invited to add his name. Then there'd be more handshakes, and shy kisses from the women, and the fluttering of white gloves in farewell.

To be fair, Neil was never quite sure how permanent was the impact he was making on town after town, but as the Wheelabout neared the end of its first week, he began to keep a diary on a small cassette recorder. The diary was dictated in chronological order — Day One, Day Two, Day Three — and a year later it makes fascinating listening.

His voice in these early days is firm, self-confident, even slightly over-bearing. The send off from Petersfield, he reports, was "excellent". At Winchester Cathedral, the Wheelabout pauses for a special service conducted by the Bishop of Basingstoke. Five musicians from Bedales play a Mozart Clarinet Quintet and a pupil from a local school reads Milton's sonnet "On his Blindness". This was obviously an occasion of some importance, yet Neil's comments on the tape are principally reserved for the ramp specially prepared for him to wheel into the cathedral. "Why" he asks, "isn't it there all the time?" Fifteen miles beyond Winchester, at Romsey, he chides the local council for "terrible pavements" and Bournemouth earns a scolding for its lack of "dropped kerbs" and over-fondness for revolving doors. Southampton City Centre, on the other hand, is "well-ramped" with "nice wide pavements" and "very accessible shops". The only irritation here is the fact that most restaurants and cafes in big stores appear to be on the second floor, a "thoughtless" piece of planning for anyone on wheels. Heading west, the Wheelabout convoy arrives in Yeovil, a town designed centuries ago for a world without wheelchairs. It is, Neil confides to his cassette recorder, "awful".

Thus, on the Wheelabout cassettes, a radically new version of the country began to take shape, defined not by antiquity or charm, or the niceness of people, but by its tolerance of the wheelchair.

At the end of the first week, Wheelabout arrived on the edge of Wales. Financially, things were going well. Each town or city yielded its own quota of cheques, and there were eager takers for the huge stock of sponsorship forms. As well, there were some novel departures in fund raising. At Blandford, boys and girls from the Clayesmore School jogged for ten miles alongside Neil to raise money, while pupils from the Cathedral School at Wells enjoyed a day out of uniform but were obliged to pay a fine of 25p each towards Wheelabout. The sheer volume of cheques, postal orders, and cash was quickly becoming a liability but Mike Mills had anticipated the problem and had asked each of the school bursars en route to collect the day's takings from Bob Slatter, and to bank it in the name of Wheelabout. In this way, Mike was able to keep a running check on totals to date, to answer the ever-growing number of enquiries from the media.

As each of the crew bedded into a particular role, Bob assumed the task of trying to keep the convoy as close to the schedule as possible. Each day, awaking in a different school, he'd rise about six for a stroll and a glimpse of his new surroundings before the day's routine began. At seven, Neil would be roused, dressed, fed, and prepared for the road. The more intimate tasks were generally left to Toni, but for once there was no lack of willing hands for transfers into and out of the wheelchair. Once on the road, it was a question of trying to make the next town in time. The vehicles were interlinked by Storno short wave radios and Bob would normally supply directions from the lead vehicle.

At lunchtime there'd be a meal in a church hall or a scout hut courtesy of the WRVS, followed by a hasty exit in time to make the next appointment. Each afternoon would end with the arrival at that night's school, and after supper Neil would generally talk to the assembled pupils while Bob got on the phone to Eileen back at Steep. She'd have been in touch during the day with Mike Mills and would have a list of the latest requests for factory visits, disabled get-togethers, or media interviews. On the basis of these appointments, Bob would then re-draft the next day's schedule and the crew would convene for a chat before bed. For Bob, each day ended with the writing of postcards. These would be mailed back to Bedales next day, where they formed part of a series of displays on Neil's carefully monitored progress round the country.

Inevitably, there were high points on the trip. The route had been planned to enable Neil to visit each of the country's spinal units, and with the exception of Stoke Mandeville — where no one seemed to know or care about Wheelabout — these sessions were especially productive. For patients with a recent spinal injury, the very sight of a C5 bending all the rules and exposing himself to a thousand miles in a wheelchair was massively therapeutic.

But there were other surprises en route, as well. On one occasion, for instance, the Wheelabout received an urgent summons to drop in on the Tarmac factory, the headquarters of the civil construction group. The convoy made the necessary detour and Bob went ahead to meet the reception committee. There he found a huge semi-circle of motorway graders, lights on and horns at the ready, waiting to greet Neil. All work had stopped to prepare this special welcome and when Neil finally wheeled around a bend in the drive there was a spontaneous roar of approval. Neil, dwarfed by the vast machines, was visibly moved and the management then insisted that they all stayed for tea. Afterwards there was a generous cheque from the bosses and the workforce, though it wasn't until they were leaving that Bob discovered the reason for all the fuss. One of the firm's secretaries was herself handicapped, and the men thought the world of her.

By the end of the second week, the Wheelabout was half way up the country on the outskirts of Manchester. By common consent, things were chaotic but fun. The only private reservations belonged to Toni. From the start, she'd had qualms about the Wheelabout. By nature she had no great affection for publicity, and she was fast becoming acutely sensitive about other people's assumptions that she was Neil's wife. Neil, who was conscious of this, went out of his way to correct the impression, but Bob was somehow unaware of the growing tension between them and continued to introduce Neil and Toni as man and wife. It was, he felt, the simplest explanation.

But the result, for Toni, was a growing sense of alienation. She'd never really belonged to Wheelabout and now she was simply outnumbered. Wherever she looked, there were Slatters: Neil, Bob, Graham and soon Eileen and Robert. Individually, she liked them all, but en masse she felt increasingly trapped. As a direct result she did most of her travelling in the support vehicle driven by Jonathan Upfold, a young friend from Petersfield who'd volunteered his services for the whole trip. This naturally grated on Neil, who monitored the relationship from the confines of his ambulance. Finally on the outskirts of Manchester, the tension between them became unbearable and it was Toni who snapped. "We were all in a garage, getting petrol, and I was sitting in the front of John's van, and Neil could see me from the ambulance, and he said over the radio, "Toni, I really don't like the way you're sitting" — because I was too close to John or whatever — and I just told him to stuff it, just like that, and he knew for once that I meant it. I deliberately didn't calm down for the rest of the day and when we got to the school that night I told him I was going to leave him. He tried everything that night — spite, tears, mind games, the lot, but I'd had enough and he knew it."

That night, the Wheelabout had come to rest at Cheethams School in Manchester. Neil was in no mood for small talk, but this sudden crisis happened to coincide with the arrival of a television film crew from Southern TV in Southampton. They'd already made plans for a half hour documentary and by prior arrangement they were to spend the next three days alongside Neil, trying to capture the real flavour of the Wheelabout. The script called for all the heroic qualities — pluck, wit, courage, charm — but as they burst into his room with their neat pre-conceptions and incessant demands, he began to wonder exactly how long he could last. Toni's news had come as a bombshell. He'd been aware of tension, certainly, but he'd been far too busy with Wheelabout to suspect that she was on the point of leaving. The fact that she'd told him, and the fact that she evidently meant it, suddenly made the whole exercise pointless. Without Toni, he was nothing. Preaching independence for the disabled was one thing. Actually doing it was quite another.

The rest of the Wheelabout, thirty eight days of it, was darkened by the shadow of Toni's impending departure. "After Manchester, we never made love. I felt very sorry for him. He had enough on his plate without me to cope with and I knew there were times when he got very pissed off. The first couple of nights after I told him, I just went off in the evening and left him with Bob or Graham. They used to sit with him a lot when he was crying. They were really good to him, much better than I could ever have been. By and large I tried to avoid being alone with him because it simply made him worse. I'd given him a definite date — the 27th July — because otherwise he'd never have believed me. I'd never have let him go into a home, but he never knew that."

For Neil, the first days after Manchester were a nightmare. The TV crew came and went, finally the wiser, and the Wheelabout headed north for Scotland. During the day he did his best to keep the misery off his face, handling the never ending civic pleasantries with deft charm. Where it mattered, he made a special effort, pleading for a particular facility, acknowledging an especially generous cheque. At stops like the Musselburgh Spinal Unit outside Edinburgh, he radiated confidence. But most of the time he'd switched onto automatic until the evenings when he could close the door on the world and its lenses, and try to come to terms with the direction his own life would now take. Toni gone was bad enough. He loved her as a person and would miss her more than he dared imagine. But she was also his lifeline, his one sure buffer against committal to a home or a long stay hospital, and in these terms the Wheelabout had suddenly become all too relevant. For Neil, the options were quite simple. Returning to Dunhill Mews, after his previous experience, would be unfair on everybody. Toni would soon be gone. That left a simple choice: either he'd find some way of staying on at Grange Road, or he'd have to face the rest of his life in an institution. The latter, he knew, was out of the question. Somehow he had to find a way of staying at Grange Road — and that, at last, would mean real independence.

On the cassette tapes, at this point, there's a very different Neil Slatter. Gone is the confidence of the first week. Instead, the voice is hesitant. Facts are forgotten, sentences left in mid-air. Somehow the voltage is down, the fire is out, and behind each slow sentence is the unvoiced suspicion that none of it really matters any more. Very little of this showed during the day. Almost permanently on duty, Neil and his wheelchair featured in a never ending sequence of newspaper, television and radio reports down Britain's east coast. He condemned access at Scarborough as "appalling". His reception at Pinderfields Spinal Unit at Wakefield he described as "tremendous". The Mayor of Rugby got a special vote of thanks "for bothering to take notes of what's needed". And the Lord Mayor of London was dismissed as "a dead loss.... just not interested... a complete waste of time".

To this degree, Neil had become a true professional: tireless, committed, articulate. But the performance was deceptive because he knew only too well that the demands of each day were simply an anaesthetic. The nights were still awful, and the fact that the rest of the family now knew didn't make anything easier. His brother, Graham, acted as a go between, and he knew Toni well enough to recognise that she meant what she said, yet he found it impossible to convince Neil. "He never really expected her to go, not until the very last moment. The last couple of evenings on the Wheelabout he was in tears and everything, terrible state. He just didn't want it to happen yet there was nothing he could do to prevent it, and it was against his nature to even try. It was awful to see."

The Wheelabout arrived back in Petersfield on the 26th June. The following day there was a triumphant entry into Portsmouth, a reception, and the usual civic speeches. Drum majorettes high-kicked for the crowd, local celebrities offered their congratulations, and Neil succumbed to yet another TV interview. The Wheelabout, he conceded, had been an extraordinary experience. He'd been amazed by reactions up and down the country. It was disgraceful that 70 per cent of Town Halls had been inaccessible to wheelchairs. He hoped he'd been able to do some permanent good. Next he was thinking of water skiing in Chichester Harbour. But now he just wanted to go home. With a smile and a wave he wheeled away across the field towards the privacy of the old ambulance, and the company of his family. Behind him trailed Toni and a couple of dogs. In exactly four weeks, she'd be gone.

Chapter Nine

The aftermath of Wheelabout was, inevitably, an anti-climax. For one thing, Neil was understandably exhausted. Fifty-four days on the road — the constant transfers in and out of the ambulance, the never ending welcomes, the hands to shake, the questions to answer, the points to make — all this had been compounded by the abrupt collapse of his relationship with Toni, and the experience had left its mark. The pair of them spent the weekend at Grange Road, Toni circling the flat, making a mental inventory of the things that needed to be done before she left while Neil sat slumped in his chair, gazing at the television. Physically, the trip had left his body drained; where it was possible to ache, he ached all the time.

The following week brought a fresh ordeal. The Southern Television documentary was nearing completion but the producer was fully aware of what was happening between Toni and Neil, and was keen that this change in their relationship should be discussed on camera. The film had set out to offer a candid account of disability and it would, he felt, be utterly wrong to ignore this major crisis in Neil's life. Neil saw the logic in this but knew the price he'd have to pay. Yet another part of him would become public property.

Toni, too, had her doubts. She was sure of her own motives for leaving Neil but knew she was also wide open to public censure. To the casual onlooker, unaware of the real implications of tetraplegia, her imminent departure was simply desertion. She was abandoning a cripple in his hour of need. For this reason, more than any other, she agreed to do the interview. "I just wanted people to know the truth — that I was leaving Neil, not his wheelchair. That was the real difference. The fact that he was disabled didn't matter. Had he not been disabled, I'd probably have left him years ago."

The interview took place in an hotel room in Petersfield, Neil and Toni side by side against a background of dark oak panels. The interviewer, James Montgomery, led them gently through the entire course of their relationship, from the early days in Guildford and Churt, through the trauma of the accident, through the long winter days of Stoke Mandeville and Steep. With total frankness, they discussed the routine humiliations of tetraplegia: the bladder problems and the condoms and the thrice-weekly manual evacuations. They described their attempts to put together some kind of sex life. They chuckled over the more bizarre episodes. They talked of the flat at Grange Road, and the experience of the Wheelabout. And at the end of it all they admitted — sadly — that the relationship had finally ground to a halt. They'd tried and they'd failed and now they'd be going their separate ways. In all, the interview took two hours. The crew, calloused by years of hard journalism, listened to every word. For them both, it was an act of remarkable courage.

The following day Neil attended a grand reception in the local Festival Hall. Petersfield's favourite son wheeled in to a fanfare from a cornet-playing schoolgirl, and from then on the evening was his. There were cakes to cut, drinks to quaff, toasts to propose, and yet more cheques to bank from a number of local sponsors. The town's Mayor thanked him for his efforts and Neil then took the microphone for the evening's keynote speech. He described the experience of the Wheelabout, where they had been, who they'd talked to, what they'd found. He reported on access problems and mobility issues, and various other forms of discrimination. He thanked his numerous local fans for their faith and support, and most important of all he made the point that the work was only just beginning. "The problems...." he said, "... are bigger than I imagined. It's going to be a very slow process for people to accept the handicapped back into society."

By any standards, it was an impressive performance. One onlooker was a social worker called Jane Mercer. She'd known Neil slightly for a few months and was soon to play an important role in his immediate future, but that night at the Festival Hall she found herself marvelling at what Neil had managed to achieve. "He's special because he works things out for himself. He knows what he wants and he has the personal knack of getting it. He's extremely bright and extremely persuasive and he doesn't give up. He has this rare ability to turn fantasies into realities. The word that comes to my mind is charisma. He has tremendous personal magnetism. It's these facets of his personality which have enabled him to face up to and accept the challenge of his severe physical handicap."

As the dust began to settle after Wheelabout, it began to dawn on

Neil that his life had taken a radically new direction. In precisely the way that Toni had hoped, the Wheelabout had made Neil's name. More than that, it had left him with a huge legacy of committments all over the country. There were letters to answer, contacts to chase up, local authorities to harass, promises to be kept. The Wheelabout fund was now topping £40,000 and that meant decisions on who should receive the first Meyra chairs. Then there were the 33 hours of cassette tapes to be transcribed, press cuttings to be filed, a book to write. And in a wider political sense, there was a war to be declared. The war would be on behalf of the country's disabled, *all* the disabled, and Neil now felt himself qualified to help direct some of the opening skirmishes. The first step would be to create coalitions of the various disabilities at local and national level. Only when that had happened did it make sense to confront the nation's various bureaucracies and demand a better deal.

But Neil's immediate battle was rather more personal. There were just three weeks left before Toni's ultimatum expired, and it was time to get his own future at Grange Road secured. Neil had already gone on record in the East Hants Post, announcing that he intended to make his own bid for real independence, and he now contacted Jane Mercer, the social worker, and put the problem squarely in her lap. She drove down from Alton to see him. "What was so unusual was that he'd already worked the whole thing out for himself. It was my role to get it for him. I was simply his agent."

Together, Neil and Jane listed the kind of help that Neil would need to survive at Grange Road without Toni. Neil had already had a Home Help for some time. It was now a question of increasing the amount of hours of Home Help to cover his daily needs and expanding the service to meet them. This required more flexibility on the part of an already overstretched scheme, but after some discussion a compromise was reached with the Home Help Organiser, Isobel Belize, and Neil was able to settle into a routine with Joanne, his existing Home Help.

The next step was arranging for his regular medical needs, including the bowel evacuations. These would need to be carried out by the District Nursing Service which was also overstretched, but their co-operation would be essential to Neil's survival. This would have to be discussed with and authorised by his GP, and Neil had already made an approach to him. With his medical and domestic needs answered, Neil was left with the residue of vital daily tasks which usually fell to Toni. These included getting him up, getting him washed, glueing on the regular condom, getting him dressed and

Neil at work on the SIA newsletter he edits from Petersfield. The tool in his right hand is known as a "plonker".

ready for the day's work at the typewriter or on the telephone or out and about. At the end of the day it also meant putting the whole process into reverse. What was needed was someone local, caring enough to work flexible hours, acting as a kind of substitute relative. In most parts of the country that would add up to an impossible demand, but in this respect Neil was exceptionally lucky because Petersfield was one of the few towns to boast a Care Attendance Scheme.

Care Attendance is a relatively new concept. It began in the mid-seventies when a viewer of the nightly television soap opera 'Crossroads' wrote in to the programme's producer and pointed out an inaccuracy in a recent episode. The episode had centred on Sandy, a cripple. Sandy had been improperly transferred from his bed to his wheelchair and the concerned viewer, himself tetraplegic, felt that it set a possibly dangerous example for others who might be watching. Intrigued by the admonition, the programme's producer visited the tetraplegic and was impressed enough to mention the incident to ATV's Chairman, Lord Grade. As a result of that conversation, a grant of £5,000 was made available for an unspecified paraplegic cause, and this money finally came to rest in Rugby, where an ex-district nurse called Pat Osborne used it to back her personal belief that many paraplegics would prefer to live at home, if only the right kind of care could be found to relieve hard pressed friends or relatives. She set up a pilot team of care attendants who looked after the kind of daily tasks that many relatives found beyond them. The scheme was a great success and attracted subsequent funding from Government and EEC sources. Now, six years later, there are twenty-four other schemes run by the Crossroads Trust.

In the wake of the Crossroads experiment, Hampshire County Council set up three pilot schemes of their own, in Basingstoke, Southampton, and South East Hants. The latter area included Petersfield, and Neil had approached Mary Hopcroft, the Area Organiser for the Care Attendance Scheme, who was very enthusiastic about his plan to survive at home and more than pleased to include him in the scheme. This would provide the last piece in the jigsaw of domiciliary care which would keep Neil out of an institution.

Jane's next step was to organise a case conference. This was hosted by Neil's GP, a New Zealander who had swopped practices with the regular GP for a year. His experience of equivalent situations in New Zealand, where independent living is less unusual, had given him a great deal of sympathy for Neil, and he was only too keen to find a way to keep Neil at Grange Road. The conference was attended by the Care Attendant Director, the Home Help Supervisor, the District Nurse, and Jane herself, and one by one they worked through Neil's needs. On all sides there was a great commitment to making the scheme work, and the conference ended with a promise from the GP that he would allow a period of three months to elapse before he made a final decision on whether or not he could permit Neil to stay at Grange Road. On paper, Neil would be taking a number of substantial risks by choosing to live alone. The various care agencies would organise the key bits of his day, but at night there were a hundred and one ways he could do himself serious damage. Most of his body was still unable to distinguish between hot or cold and there was a consequent danger of scalds or burns. Any chest infection from a minor cold upwards was a potential hazard because he lacked the muscular control to sneeze properly or get rid of catarrh. Likewise, he'd be in serious danger of choking to death if — for any reason — he should start being sick. Flat on his back, there was simply no way he could move. These risks Neil was willing to accept. "The really new thing was my preparedness to spend nights alone. Many severely handicapped people are frightened of that. They want round-the-clock care but I knew that was far too expensive. As long as I could have a phone by the bed, I was willing to take the risk. In that respect I was lucky. Some people can't use a phone."

Some of these hazards could be minimised by further adaptations to the flat, and at this point Jane called in Clare McKenna, the Senior Advisor for Disablement and Rehabilitation at the Social Services HQ at Winchester. Already a fan of Neil's she drove across to Petersfield, and together with Toni and Neil she inspected the flat. Toni had already made a list of important adaptations, and these Clare passed on to David Hooper, the District Council Housing Officer, with a recommendation that they be put in hand as soon as possible.

In Clare's view, the adaptations were twofold. Firstly, Neil needed far better access within the flat. That meant knocking out some of the existing doorways and creating wide, arched throughways between the various rooms, ideal for the passage of Neil's wheelchair. Secondly, there were a number of changes to be done in the bathroom: lever taps, a new wash basin, and the installation of an anti-scald thermostat in the airing cupboard. With these adaptations complete, the flat would — in Clare's view — be safe.

Hooper studied the list and put it out to tender. The selected estimate costed the adaptations at £1,180 and Council approval was obtained for work to begin. From Neil's point of view, the only big drawback was the forfeit of his rights as a tenant to buy the property. Under Government legislation, local councils are not obliged to sell specially adapted accommodation.

As Neil's new life began to take shape, Jane Mercer could only admire his tenacity. "As social workers we are normally battling for

The Family

our clients against the various systems and bureaucracies, but with
Neil there's very little battle to be fought. People bend over backwards
to help him — perhaps because of his personality, perhaps because
he's achieved a certain reputation for getting things done. Maybe in
some ways he's *too* successful. Other disabled people may start to ask
why *he's* so special, but hopefully he'll be able to turn the situation to
their advantage as well as his own."

In two and a half weeks, mid-July, Neil had now secured himself at
least three months grace. The Care Attendance scheme, plus the
supporting programme of daily help, was to run until the end of
October — at which point it would be reviewed. If it was judged a
success, he then had a firm promise that it would be made permanent.
In the meantime, Toni was still in residence, making final adjustments
to the flat before she left. On all drawers and cupboards, she screwed
loops of chain to give Neil easier access. The fridge she installed waist
high on a shelf in the kitchen for the same reason. Emotionally, Neil
had now accepted the fact that Toni really was going to leave him, and
that life would go on without her. In one sense the loss was just as
savage as it had ever been, but in another he'd begun to look forward to

the challenge of real independence. "I suppose it was the logical conclusion of what we'd been saying on Wheelabout. That the disabled should have the choice — and the chance — to look after themselves, to control their own lives, to make their own decisions, to take a few risks again... emotionally or in any other sense."

Members of Neil's family felt very much the same way. No one blamed Toni for wanting to leave. On the contrary, Eileen insisted that she'd always think of her as "one of us". But making Neil face the reality of life on his own was an opportunity, not a handicap. Brother Robert, for one, had no doubts. "Toni leaving was the best thing that ever happened to Neil. She'd been fantastic to him all that time, God knows why, but now he really had to work it all out for himself. The difference that made is amazing. It made him *really* strong. Not just a good bullshitter, but *really* strong."

At this stage, Jane Mercer did a detailed analysis of Neil's personal finances. Without Toni to help him, the responsibility for meeting his bills would be exclusively his. Neil's income came from three sources, all of them state funded. After Toni's departure his invalidity pension would bring him £38.10 a week. This was meant to cover his food and accommodation costs. Another £22.65 came in the shape of a non-taxable attendance allowance to enable him to cover the costs incurred by the need for extra care. The third weekly grant, a mobility allowance to cover his transport costs, yielded £14.50. In all, Neil was therefore receiving £75.25 per week. [1]

Of this, £18.14 went on his rent, £12.00 on gas and electricity, £26.00 on food. £6.57 on TV and video. £1.00 on life assurance and £1.00 on a weekly contribution towards his Home Help. His telephone was paid for by the Social Services and the Spinal Injuries Association, for whom he now worked as Secretary of the Hampshire and District Group. In all, Neil was therefore left with a weekly balance of just over ten pounds to spend as he wished. It wasn't a fortune, but Jane Mercer knew many families who had to get by on considerably less.

Toni left Grange Road, on schedule, at the end of July. As well as helping Neil prepare for a new life, she'd spent the previous month making arrangements of her own, and had surprised herself by finding a job, transport, and somewhere to live. The job was on the Butser Hill Iron Age Farm, an enterprising educational development in the Queen Elizabeth Country Park, a few miles south of Petersfield. There, she was to advise on access and facilities for the disabled, as well as lend a

1 *At 1981 rates.*

125

more general hand with the animals and the farm work. An advertisement in the local paper had secured her a flat nearby, and she'd also been able to acquire a small motor bike for evening and weekend trips into Petersfield. One of Neil's last presents to her was a brand new crash helmet.

Toni left Grange Road with few regrets. Of course, it was impossible not to feel sorry for Neil but in many ways the decision to leave was four years overdue. She'd delayed leaving him in the first place because he'd nearly died, and she'd stayed on because learning how to live again was a very slow process. Now he'd got himself this far — nationally known, well taken care of — she felt justified in going her own way. "I suppose I just felt sod it, I've done my bit, the next couple of years are mine, you've got enough on your plate to take care of. The problem in the end was that we were two different people. Neil's emotional. He needs all that stuff. I'm just nervous. I need room…"

With Toni gone, and a lot of help from Pat Saunders and Mary Jordan, two local paraplegics, Neil surrounded himself with a barricade of work. On behalf of the Spinal Injuries Association, he had expanded the newsletter to a regular sixteen-page edition. As editor, designer, typist, and principal contributor, this kept him more than busy. On top of that, there were still Wheelabout cheques coming in, and he made his way to a number of presentations from scout groups, fire brigades, and the like. The first Wheelabout chairs were also due for delivery and this meant trips as far afield as Newcastle where the chairs were made the centre of a formal handing-over ceremony. For the time being, Neil still had access to the Wheelabout ambulance, 'Gloria' but this was soon to be reclaimed, leaving him once again at the mercy of other people's goodwill.

As the fine weather finally arrived, Neil also kept the publicity pot on the boil. The Wheelabout had taught him a great deal about the media's addiction to the bizarre or the unusual, and he had no objections to exploiting this weakness if it meant a few more column inches on the real problems of the disabled. Thus, on the 20th August, the East Hants Post announced Neil's latest wheeze: a water skiing trip in a wheelchair. As a stunt it was hardly new, and he'd already mentioned the idea at the end of Wheelabout, but the paper thought enough of the story to make it their front page lead. To date Neil has still to fulfill his promise, and he occasionally admits that he may never do so, but in a sense the project has already served its purpose: the 'Post' article also reminded readers that the Wheelabout fund was still open, and that the disabled still needed access, housing, mobility, education and employment.

Another important departure for Neil was the development of his counselling activities. His own response to counselling had convinced him of the value of this kind of therapy, and he'd begun to counsel other local paraplegics with more recent injuries than his own. For this work, Neil appeared to have a natural aptitude. Before the accident, he'd been extremely deft at establishing intimate relationships. He had a natural instinct for the mood and feelings of other people, and a year on his back had given him plenty of time to develop this gift. The results, for people like Jane Mercer, could be startling. "Neil has developed a hyper-sensitivity as a person. He seems to know at once how others feel — about themselves and about him — perhaps because his very existence depends on this acuity. So I'll walk into his living room and he'll know at once how I feel. It's almost alarming. Unlike most clients, he doesn't accept the client role. He wants to know about *you*. Maybe that's part of his defence mechanism. He's very difficult to know."

Aware of this potency in counselling situations, Neil attended a weekend counselling course in Coventry. The course was designed to explore the emotional and sexual problems of the disabled, a challenge which Neil readily accepted. He submitted to a long counselling session, admitted to a sense of incompleteness after Toni's departure, but came away with a clutch of new contacts. One of them, a young occupational therapist called Christine, soon became his girlfriend. She began to travel down from the Midlands to Petersfield for weekends at Grange Road, an arrangement which drew a surprising response from Toni.

By now, after a decent interval, Toni was making occasional reappearances at Neil's to chat, or cook him a meal, and the arrival of another woman in Neil's life took her completely by surprise — much to Eileen's amusement. "Chris had come for the weekend and I was down there on a Saturday morning and quite suddenly Toni came in, completely out of the blue. I'm afraid it was quite obvious that Chris had spent the night with Neil but Toni didn't turn a hair. She'd brought a bottle of wine for Neil, and she was laughing and joking and somehow she just took the place over. It was extraordinary, I'd never seen anything like it. They went out at midday, all of them, and Toni was sitting on Neil's knee going into the town, just like old times. Later Toni told me how jealous she'd felt. Of Chris."

By this time, the end of November, Neil's three month trial period

Toni and Neil

was coming to an end. By common consent it had been completely successful, and Neil's GP didn't even bother with the formality of reconvening the case conference before announcing that the arrangement had his blessing. From that day on, Neil's future was secure, and he now turned his attention to pursuing the logic of the Wheelabout, to exploring ways in which he might broaden that single initiative and take up a still wider cause. Where that road may take him provides the substance of the last chapter.

Chapter Ten

"An entire social movement arose over the question of where certain people must sit when they ride the bus. Big deal. I can't even get on the bus..."

Frank Labinowitz, 36
San Diego, California (C5)

Until very recently, the notion that people like Neil — paraplegics or tetraplegics — might one day be "cured" has been regarded as a rather cruel joke. Since 1978 though, there have been signs that research may have transformed future prospects for the spinally injured. The Americans in particular have been launching a number of research programmes to find ways of returning some degree of sensation or control to the nation's paralysed and their findings have led to a new mood of optimism. After a 1981 Conference, organised by a body then known as the Paralysis Cure Research Foundation, it was claimed that a cure for paralysis *will* be found, possibly within the next ten years.

In the broadest terms, research has been developing in two separate areas. Firstly, scientists have been trying to find ways of minimising paralysis immediately after the point of injury. If the spinal cord has been completely severed, this is out of the question, but one of the difficulties of treating severe spinal injuries is trying to establish whether or not this has happened.

The first reaction of the spinal cord to injury is a condition known as "spinal shock", a total loss of function below the point of impact. Occasionally this paralysis will be brief, no more than half an hour, in which case it's known as "spinal concussion". But more often spinal shock will last for as long as 72 hours, during which period the doctors can't be at all sure of the real extent of the damage. One view, of course, is to operate immediately, but operations on the spine carry a real risk of further damage and may jeopardise the cord's chances of natural recovery. For this reason, most UK consultants prefer to wait and see, though American surgeons routinely operate on recently injured patients in a bid to limit paralysis.

This decision — whether or not to operate — is a cause of fundamental disagreement between English and American doctors. But what's become more increasingly obvious to researchers is the

129

critical importance of what happens to the spinal cord during the first four hours after injury. The cord is encased within the spinal column. Between the corset of bone, and the cord itself, there are also a series of surprisingly tough membranes. The cord's natural response to severe injury is to swell. This swelling, plus the body's secretion of adrenalin-like chemicals called "vaso-constricters", cuts off the blood supply. Without blood and vital oxygen, all or part of the injured segment of spinal cord will die. One answer, then, is to try and find a way of inhibiting this process.

Research has so far suggested a number of solutions. One is to somehow block the body's secretion of vaso-constricters, thus reducing swelling and minimising long-term damage. A second treatment is to cool the injured segment of spinal cord, slowing down the body's metabolic rate and thus reducing swelling. This is the same principle first-aiders use on normal bruising, and is relatively uncomplicated. Researchers at New York University Medical Center have been trying to achieve the same metabolic effect by the use of steroid drugs, and Naloxone is now administered in the federally funded Spinal Trauma Units in the USA. A last technique, pioneered in Australia, is to give the patient pressurised oxygen in a hyperbaric oxygen chamber. The latter resembles a diving decompression chamber and by breathing a special atmosphere, heavy with oxygen, the injured tissues receive a correspondingly rich dose of the life-giving gas. All these treatments, though, depend on speed. The patient must be in the right medical hands within four hours of injury if the treatment is to be given any chance of success. In densely populated countries, like the UK, this is often more than possible. Neil was lying in Guildford Hospital within an hour of falling off his motor bike.

As well as the immediate treatment of spinal injury (known in the trade as "acute" care), researchers have also been investigating ways of trying to cure chronic, or long-term, paralysis. Large parts of the medical establishment are understandably cautious of raising patients' hopes unduly high, but the onward rush of technology does appear to be offering the chance of major advances. The spinal cord remains a very complex structure but the fact that only a tenth of its millions of nerves need to be regenerated to allow a paraplegic person to walk is itself a source of great excitement. At the time of writing, there are a number of promising techniques under development.

One of them is the search for a substance which will assist in the process of regenerating the nerve cells. The spinal cords of fish and ground squirrels do regenerate, and research is being carried out in an effort to extract a substance or to produce a chemical agent which will assist in the regeneration of the spinal cord in man.

Other researchers feel that the scar tissue which forms after injury to the spinal cord acts as a bar to regeneration and so scientists are trying to remove this scar tissue or to make it pliable and penetrable. One promising approach in this field involves the replacement of the scar tissue with peripheral nerve tissue from elsewhere in the body. Unlike the nerves of the spinal cord and brain, peripheral nerves have the ability to regenerate, and experiments on rats and cats in Montreal and Leeds have indicated that the nerves of the spinal cord *do* begin to grow again as long as they can use the medium of the peripheral nerve graft. This discovery has caused a great deal of excitement within the medical world but researchers have yet to demonstrate that the nerves can reconnect successfully enough to re-establish function in man.

A third approach, under development at Harvard University, is to use synthetic substances, chiefly polymers, as a growth path for injured nerves. This, too, has so far been restricted to experiments in animals.

Another research team at New York's Columbia University believes that a considerable amount of regenerative growth could be restored to humans by means of electrical stimulation. They can already increase the rate at which human peripheral nerves regenerate, and these skills are now being applied to the spinal cord.

The micro-chip also offers enormous potential in the re-establishment of control and doctors at London's Maudsley Hospital have already been experimenting with control of the bladder by means of an implant susceptible to radio frequency stimulation. This in itself does nothing to restore the power of movement, but freedom from condoms, leg bags, and all the other apparatus of incontinence, would be a huge advance for the spinally injured, given the adequate provision of specially adapted public lavatories for the disabled.

Perhaps the most exciting of all though, is a research project currently under way at America's Wright State University in Dayton, Ohio. There, Professor Jerrold Petrofsky has developed a computer-controlled technique which permits the paralysed muscles of the body to work entirely independent of the brain. Based on a sophisticated system of electro-stimulation and feedback, Petrofsky's technique re-establishes smooth control over long-paralysed muscles and has led to the first visible evidence that paralysis caused by spinal injury may

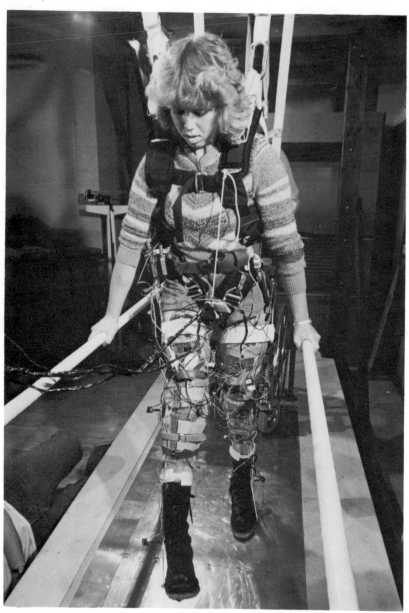

Nan Davis, a 22 year old American paraplegic, under computer control in the laboratories of Wright State University, Ohio. Nan walked for the first time on 11th November, 1982

not be as permanent as the medical establishment has so far assumed. Over the course of 1982, Professor Petrofsky successfully demonstrated that tetraplegics, paralysed for many years, could operate exercise machines with their legs, pedal stationary bicycles, and even ride adapted tricycles around the University campus. Then, on the 11th November 1982, Petrofsky astonished assembled TV crews and press men by enabling Nan Davis, a 22 year old paraplegic, to walk again. Nan had been paralysed after a car accident on her High School graduation night. On a cold November morning in Ohio, she took her first cautious steps towards a near-normal life.

For people like Neil, though, the possibility of a cure for paralysis is the most distant of prospects, something to be stored away and treated with the greatest caution. Better, for the time being, to regard paralysis as a social problem, something handed to us all by the doctors whose responsibility ends at the moment of discharge from hospital. Back in society, the real battle is for a life worth living.

For Neil, as for many other handicapped, this battle is never ending. Charm, cunning, and sheer persistence have won him the right to live under his own roof, and his electric wheelchair has given him certain freedoms in the world outside, but these are partial victories and he still faces the same problems of employment, access, mobility, housing, education and social acceptance as every other disabled person.

Take work, for instance. Recently, Neil was invited to apply for a temporary administrative job. The job involved collating research material. It was to be based at an office 16 miles away and it was to last for six months. The immediate problems were obvious. Neil had to find transport for the daily thirty-two mile round trip, he had to be sure he could get into the building and move around inside it, he had to know if his desk would be high enough for his wheelchair, that help would be available if he needed his leg bag emptying, and a million and one other tiny details that able bodied people take for granted.

In the event, though, he got no further than the interview. "I wheeled into the office and came to a stop in front of the desk. There were three men behind it. At that stage no one actually explained what the job involved so I asked to see the job description. One of the men behind the table handed me a piece of paper and I reached to take it. As I did so, I had a spasm in my hand and I dropped the paper. One of the interviewers watching leapt on this. "Look..." he said, "... you can't even use your hands." I explained about the spasm and so on but it made no difference. If I couldn't use my hands, what would I do about a telephone? How would I be able to write? I did my best to explain I could do both, and I showed them how I managed with a telephone, but the damage had been done. I was disabled. My hands didn't work like ordinary hands. The implication was I'd be too much trouble to them. Afterwards, thinking about it, I got very angry because this attitude is a very common response. It happens all the time. But it's based on a lack of awareness of the real potential of a handicapped employee. Adapting things like access and desks and so forth is no problem. As long as the money's available, that can be solved. But the big crunch comes when you realise that the real problem is attitudes — and money doesn't change that. People just assume we're different. Give anyone a wheelchair, or a white stick, and they're somehow alienated and outcast. Should appearances count for everything?"

Experiences like these confirm Neil's belief that real change will only come if disabled people band themselves together and become a true political force. "In the end it's going to be votes that count. There are more than five million disabled in this country and they all have the best possible reason for getting things changed. It's their lives at stake, the quality of their lives, and that should be enough to make us stick together. The most important thing about the International Year of Disabled People wasn't the money raising, or the improvements in access, or any of those things, but the awareness amongst the disabled that they have a right to speak out and decide how best to run their own lives."

For Neil, and others like him, the task now is to take advantage of this new mood and to maintain the momentum. Locally he's helped to form the East Hants Coalition, a coming-together of the area's disabled in the belief that strength lies in numbers. "Locally, we're looking for 100 per cent involvement. A coalition of disabilities should bring everyone together for the common good. The Council's Public Library Committee should be able to come to us and say "What do you need?" In which case we'd be able to say we need a ramp to get into the building, and electrically opening doors, and wide aisles, and low shelves, and if it's a two storey building, we need a lift. Then for the blind we need braille signs, and raised buttons on the lifts, and flashing fire alarms for the deaf, and specially located seats for respiratory sufferers, etc.. A coalition provides the focus for all these problems. It's politically quite dangerous because it leaves councils with no excuse for not taking us into account. We're speaking with one voice."

At national level, Neil is helping to apply the same principle. In November 1981 he attended the formation of the British Council of

Organisations of Disabled People (BCODP), a coalition of all the disabilities including such bodies as the Association of Blind and Partially Sighted Students and Teachers, the Union of Physically Impaired Against Segregation (UPIAS) and the Spinal Injury Association. Some twenty national organisations, each of which is self-run, representing thousands of disabled people, jointly asserted their right to represent themselves on the circuit of international and other conferences which provide a talking shop for the discussion of disability. The coalition met on the seventh of November and promptly sent a three-person delegation to Singapore for a meeting of the Disabled Peoples' International (DPI). Conferences like these are normally regarded as the prerogative of able-bodied delegates, a policy for which Neil has little time. "It's completely wrong. They don't send us because some of us have to take a helper and that doubles the cost. Yet the fact is that some of us have a genuine contribution to make. We're not saying that because we're disabled, we're automatically the experts, but some of us have worked very hard to gain a lot of knowledge, and it's very frustrating to be unable to take the process any further. It's hard enough as it is, without yet more handicaps. Sometimes I get to thinking it's our role to accept what we're given and keep our mouths shut."

Underterred, Neil now spends most of his time continuing to harry local authorities, government departments and anyone else who chooses to listen, about a range of specific issues — a process which is all the more effective because it now has the backing of hard fact. "Take housing, for instance, it's my belief that every disabled person should have the right to choose how — and where — he or she should live. Some disabled want to stay in residential homes. Others don't. They want a place of their own. In principle, of course, that's fine and everyone agrees, but the housing officials point out it's impractical because it costs too much. But that's not true. Take my case. If I was in residential care, it would cost the state nearly £200 a week — and that would be one of the cheaper homes. In some local authority homes in London it's nearer £350 a week. As it is, I get under £80 a week benefit. Then the state pays for my care attendant and home help. That's £28 a week (fourteen hours at £2 an hour) and £14 a week (seven hours at £2 an hour). That makes £112 a week, nearly half the cost of residential care. Of course, they'll say that my flat needed adapting, and they're right. But that's a capital cost (approximately £4,000) and once it's done it's there forever. Whichever way you look at it, it's actually cheaper to let people live independently — if that's the way they want to live. All we're asking for is the right to choose."

Slowly, Neil is becoming aware of a new mood amongst Britain's disabled but his real inspiration still comes from the USA. "In America, things are very different. There, they've always believed in their rights as disabled people, and they've fought for those rights. They've staged huge parades, and stopped traffic and occupied government buildings just to let the rest of America know about their demands. And it worked. They've now got laws that give the disabled the right to work, and the means to work, and proper transport, and education in the same schools as the able-bodied. There you can't discriminate against the handicapped any more. It's illegal. Here it's different. They pass laws, but the laws have no teeth. It's often just lip service."

America is also the home of the fabled Centres for Independent Living (CILs). The first CIL was established in the early seventies on the UCLA Campus at Berkeley, California, and is still a mecca for visiting handicapped from all over the world. The movement was begun by Ed Roberts, a young polio victim who later became head of California's Department of Rehabilitation and the idea has now been copied nationwide. Each centre is funded on so-called "soft money" — one-off grants, loans, and the occasional legacy — and is run by the disabled themselves. Help of all kinds is available to any disabled caller and the key disability issues — work, housing, mobility, access, health maintenance — have thus been removed from the hands of the doctors. Neil, like many of his fellow disabled, thoroughly approves.

"What we have in mind are British versions of the American CILs. We think that's the best way of giving handicapped people the chance to lead independent lives, out in the community. The people we're trying to reach are the ones who are isolated or segregated or in other ways alienated from mainstream society. Wherever possible, we'll try and make use of present facilities — but where none exist, we'll try and provide them. We need to offer a whole range of services — counselling, legal advice, education, employment opportunities, help with a housing problem, liaison with council authorities and voluntary organisations, wheelchair repairs, anything at all. By setting up such services within a CIL we'll be able to help people with disabilities plan and implement the decisions which affect their lives. That way they can *really* be independent. That may sound idealistic but it's not. CILs are already being set up in Hampshire, Derbyshire, Norwich and Devon, and there are other groups under discussion. The future looks positively rosy!"

For Neil, then, the immediate future is a very full diary. On the backwash from Wheelabout, and in response to subsequent invitations, he visits schools, colleges, prisons, local councils, Womens Institute gatherings, spreading his own vision of where the disabled should be going. On the personal level he offers a compelling story; politically, the implications of what he has to say are sometimes hard to take. Sympathy, he quickly concedes, is not enough. And to give the disabled the kind of chance they want ("want... not deserve") is going to cost more than money. It's going to mean the painful revision of a number of personal attitudes, but now the initiative lies squarely with the disabled themselves. "Things aren't going to change overnight. It's going to be slow. We know that. We need a movement, like the Civil Rights Movement in America, which will feed on itself, spreading and spreading, until we're too big to ignore. And it's starting to happen. There's a new breed of disabled people, articulate, educated, prepared to stand up and speak for themselves. That's the real change, that's what I'm about. It's my job to kick arses and open eyes. We want to take part — not just in society, but in this whole battle to try and rejoin it. We want to prove we can contribute and the best way of doing that is to conduct the battle ourselves. By going out and talking to kids. By going on telly. By making a nuisance of ourselves. By laughing at ourselves and at our handicaps. People sometimes ask me why society should bother with us and I always tell them it's because it's our society as well as theirs. We're individuals, human beings. We've got something to offer. Like it or not, we *belong.*"

Neil's is a story which has touched a number of lives, some of them intimately, some of them less so. Beyond dispute, the major role belongs to the women in his life, to Toni and Eileen.

For Toni, the experience of the last four years has been invaluable. "Being with Neil has changed me completely. When I met him I was a mess. By staying with him I've become a me which is a damn sight better than the me before. I've matured a lot. I'm more stable. I made a lot of mistakes early, but at least I corrected them early. Neil's done that for me, just being with him. He's an incredible bloke, if you can handle him."

Eileen too, has no doubts that what's happened to Neil has altered the course of the lives around her. "I think our lives, Bob's and mine, have completely changed. In one sense we'll never be able to do the things we'd saved up to do, or go to the places we've wanted to go, by ourselves, once the kids are off our hands, because there'll always be Neil down the road. But that doesn't matter because we're all so much closer now. Neil's accident has actually created a relationship between Neil and his father that simply wasn't there before and it's brought us all much closer together. Before, we were drifting apart. Now we're a real family again. Who'd have thought that four years ago?"

For Neil, looking back is something he generally tries to avoid. But there are odd occasions when the past comes flooding back — the frustrations, the rage, the sheer helplessness of it all — and it's then that he finds it difficult to appreciate the distance he's covered since. Recently, for instance, there was a battery problem on his wheelchair. It was January, half past seven in the evening. Neil had decided on a trip to the pub and had wheeled around the flat collecting the dog, and his wallet, and the tartan rug with the hole in the middle which Eileen had made him as a cape for outdoor trips in the wheelchair. Finally he phoned the care attendant and asked her to come round at half past eleven. Then he headed for the back door out from the living room into the garden. Half way through the door, though, the electrics failed, and for the next four hours, Neil sat patiently in his chair waiting for a chance visitor, or his late night appointment with the care attendant, to get back in the warm. By the time help arrived, the temperature was down to minus four. Not much changes, he thought to himself, unless you keep at it.

Postscript

Throughout the writing of this book, there's one thing about Neil which has baffled me. Despite endless conversations with him and his friends, sessions with his family, and access to all the other sources which might have helped, I've found it very hard to understand his total lack of bitterness. Had I broken my neck I would have viewed the accident and its aftermath with profound resentment. Yet not once, to my knowledge, has Neil enquired why the accident should have happened to him, and not to someone else; or why the accident should have led to a broken neck and not — as in the case of the pillion passenger — to some less serious injury.

This has perplexed me since the day we met, and I'm not much closer to a solution now than I was a year ago. Perhaps it's something to do with his family and his upbringing: close, warm, secure, affectionate. Perhaps it has something to do with his less attractive traits: his doggedness, his self-belief, the sheer size of his ego. Or perhaps it's his sense of humour.

Very recently we were both sitting in a Petersfield pub called The Red Lion. We'd spent a couple of hours swopping stories, toying with various titles for the book, and downing large quantities of a local brew called Strong's Country Ale. Towards the end of the evening a girl joined us, an ex-schoolfriend of Neil's. It may be they'd once had a relationship. I don't know. In any event, we started talking about the book again. After a while the girl looked Neil in the eye and asked him what he *really* felt about being disabled. Her tone of voice suggested it was a question she'd been saving up for years. Neil laid his beer mug carefully on the table and gazed into the middle distance for a while. Then he turned back to her. He was smiling. "It's very simple" he said, "I'm just an able bodied guy who happens to do a lot of sitting down..."

Appendix 1

Organisations offering help and advice to the Disabled.

Aidis Trust
Willowbrook, Swanbourne Road, Mursley, Milton Keynes, Bucks. MK17 0JA
Provides sophisticated electronic aids for severely handicapped and elderly people.

Arts and Disability Information Service
2 Quermore Close, Bromley, Kent, BR1 4EL.

Association of Disabled Professionals
General Secretary: Peggy M. Marchant
The Stables, 73 Pound Road, Banstead, Surrey, SM7 2HU.
(07373 52366)
The Association is a self-help group seeking to improve the rehabilitation of disabled people. Members can help other members with advice on education/training and employment problems. Publishes an irregular Newsletter and a House Bulletin. Its committee, HOPE, provides information to people who have had to give up professional careers and must work at home.

British Council of Disabled People (BCODP)
5 Crowndale Road, London NW1 1TU. (01 388 6840)
National and International representation of handicapped people in Britain. Covering all areas of independent integrated living.

British Sports Association for the Disabled
Stoke Mandeville Stadium, Harvey Road, Aylesbury, Bucks. 0296 84848

Chariot
17 Wood Lane, Sutton Coldfield, West Midlands, B74 3LP.
Provides transport for severely disabled and chairfast people in the Midlands.

Association of Crossroads Care Attendant Schemes Trust Ltd.
Chief Exec. Officer: Mrs. Pat Osborne
11 Whitehall Road, Rugby, Warwickshire CV21 3AQ.
0788 61536

A similar trust operates in Scotland.
Director: Mr. A.G. Murray
24 George Square, Glasgow G2 1EG.
041 226 3793

Dial UK
Dial House, 117 High Street, Clay Cross, Derbyshire.
0246 864498

The Disability Alliance
21 Star Street, London W2 1QB.
A federation of 60 organisations of/for disabled people. The Alliance's primary aim is to introduce a comprehensive approach to financing disability, replacing the existing patchwork of social security benefits with a rational scheme based on severity of disability alone. It also encourages take-up of existing benefits with its annual Handbook and Welfare Rights information service, and publishes research reports on specific problems of disability.

Disabled Drivers Association (DDA)
Ashwellthorpe Hall, Ashwellthorpe, Norwich NR16 1EX.
050 841 449
The Association will help and advise physically disabled people, whether drivers or not, on all matters of mobility including vehicles and conversions, ferry concessions, insurance, legal requirements and government and local authority help. The DDA publishes a quarterly magazine 'Magic Carpet' which is free to members. The DDA also actively campaigns for improved government help in the mobility field and for improved facilities for the disabled. The headquarters, Ashwellthorpe Hall, is also a holiday centre set in 18 acres of ground providing ideal accommodation for wheelchair members of the DDA; for non-members there is a slight extra charge.

Disabled Drivers' Motor Club Limited
1A Dudley Gardens, Ealing, London N13 9LU.
01 840 1515
The Club will offer help and advice on motoring problems, ferry concessions, conversions, etc.. The aims of the Club are generally to protect the interests and welfare of disabled drivers. The £3.00 annual subscription entitles members to ferry concessions, discounts on insurance, reduced RAC subscriptions and a variety of services including a bi-monthly magazine. In addition there is a 24-hour answering service.

Disabled Living Foundation
346 Kensington High Street, London W14 8NS.
01 602 2491
The DLF is a charitable trust concerned with all disabilities (mental, physical and sensory) including multiple handicaps and the infirmities of age. The Foundation works to help disabled people in those aspects of ordinary life which present special problems and difficulties. Its activities

embrace a comprehensive information service, a permanent collection of aids of all kinds, and incontinence and clothing advisory services. Other studies made by the Foundation include sport and physical recreation, music, gardening, employment, further education and the problems of those with partial sight.

Disablement Income Group (DIG) & Disablement Income Group Charitable Trust
Attlee House, 28 Commercial Street, London E1 6LR.
01 247 2128

Disablement Income Group (Scotland)
152 Morrison Street, Edinburgh EH3 8BY
031 228 1666
DIG is a pressure group, with local branches, campaigning for legislative reform to provide adequate experience in providing a bridge into a wider friendship circle. They also provide an advisory service on benefits.

Electronic Aids Loan Service for Disabled People
Roger M. Jefcoate, Willowbrook, Swanbourne Road, Mursley, Milton Keynes, Bucks. MK17 0JA
0296 72 533
Free loans for limited periods. Also free independent advice on all types of electronic aids.

Environment for the Handicapped, Centre on
126 Albert Street, London NW1 7NF
01 482 2247
Planning and advice on architecture

Gardens for the Disabled Trust
Miss P. Tallents, Moor Green, Wittersham, Isle of Oxney, Kent
Encourages disabled people to enjoy gardening as a creative hobby; advice and information; newsletter; garden club.

Greater London Association for the Disabled (GLAD)
1 Thorpe Close, London W10 5XL
01 960 5799
Aims to be a source of authoritative information on local and national welfare legislation, and to press for improvements in the quality of life of disabled Londoners. It publishes a directory of clubs in London for physically disabled people, a quarterly magazine and other specialist publications.

Hampshire Centre for Independent Living (HCIL)
4 Plantation Way, Bordon, Hants. GU35 9HD
To help people with disabilities plan and implement decisions that affect their lives. To enable persons with disabilities to live independently in the community and to integrate 'friends' of disabled people.

Ileostomy Association of Great Britain, Northern Ireland and Eire
Amblehurst House, Chobham, Woking, Surrey GU23 8PZ
09905 8277
Founded in 1956 by a few ileostomists who saw a need for mutual self-help. Members are provided with advice and encouragement in the pre- and post-operative periods. There is a network of divisions and branches throughout Britain, including three divisions in Scotland. The Association has a welfare fund to assist members who find themselves in financial difficulties, and honorary welfare officers can help and advise with personal problems. A quarterly journal is sent free of charge to all members.

Independent Disabled Self Sufficiency Association
7 Alfred Street, Bath, Avon BA1 2QU.
0225 25197
Advice and information (send s.a.e.); publishes quarterly journal 'Phoenix'.

John Grooms Association for the Disabled
10 Gloucester Drive, London N4 2LP
01 802 7272
Provides care and accommodation for severely disabled people and elderly ladies. Runs a craft centre with associated homes on a garden estate at Edgware; holiday hotels for wheelchair users in Somerset and North Wales, and self-catering holiday units on sites in other areas. Through a housing association promotes the provision of purpose-built flats for disabled people.

Leonard Cheshire Foundation
26-29 Maunsel Street, London SW1P 2QN
01 828 1822
Provides residential accommodation and a wide range of activities for severely disabled or chronically sick people (mainly up to the age of 60 on first admission). Short term accommodation is normally available. Publishes quarterly journal, 'Cheshire Smile'.

Mobility Information Service
Copthorne Community Hall, Shelton Road, Shrewsbury, Shropshire
0743 68383
Information on cars, adaptations, costs, etc.

Mobility International
2 Colombo Street, London SE1 8DP
01 928 2755

Mobility for the Disabled, Joint Committee on
Hon. Sec: Jill Vernon
c/o ASBAH, Tavistock House, Tavistock Square, London WC1H 9HJ.

Motability
The Adelphi, John Adam Street, London WC2N 6AZ
01 839 5191

Northern Ireland Committee for the Handicapped (NICH)
2 Annalade Avenue, Belfast, VT7 3JH
0232 64011
NICH is a sub-committee of the Northern Ireland Council of Social Services and provides a forum for voluntary and statutory organisations working for the disabled. Its principal aims are to focus attention on the needs of handicapped people and the services available to them, to encourage discussion and concerted action by all concerned with the welfare of handicapped people in Northern Ireland to assist member organisations. It has recently set up an information service and has launched a series of booklets on holidays, sport, rehabilitation services and access.

Omega Assurance Services
30 Beamhill Road, Burton-on-Trent, Staffs. DE13 4EA
0283 62596
Insurance advice by/for people with disabilities

Open University
Richard Tomlinson, Disabled Students' Officer, PO Box 48, Milton Keynes MK7 6AB
Home study and courses specially for disabled students.

Opportunities for the Disabled
1 Bank Building, Punies Street, London EC2R 8EU
Employment agency

Outset
30 Craven Street, London WC2
01 930 4255
Outset is a national charity one of whose functions is in the field of disablement. Its main activity is to carry out identification surveys of the handicapped on behalf of government departments, local authorities, area health authorities, community health councils and any other organisations concerned about the implementation of the Chronically Sick and Disabled Persons Act 1970. Outset will either act in an advisory capacity to someone wishing to carry out a survey, or construct and supervise surveys on behalf of the applicant, providing relevant training, conducting the analysis of all data, and publishing this material in report form at the end of the processing period. A fee is charged on the basis of £100 per 1000 households surveyed. A Disablement Information Unit is also now in operation, the duties of which include monitoring the progress of local authorities since the implementation of the Chronically Sick and Disabled Persons Act.

Paraplegic Association, Scottish
3 Cargil Terrace, Edinburgh, EH5 3ND
031 552 8459

Physically Handicapped and Able Bodied (PHAB)
42 Devonshire Street, London W1N 1LN
01 637 7475

Northern Ireland Branch: c/o *Northern Ireland Association of Youth Clubs, Hampton House, Glenmachan Road, Belfast, BT4 2NN. 0232 768603*
This is a national organisation concerned with the integration of physically handicapped and able bodied young people, largely through leisure activities. There are now over 360 clubs throughout the United Kingdom aiming towards equal numbers of both groups; the able-bodied being enrolled as full members rather than as "helpers". The clubs provide a setting in which barriers can be overcome and relationships established through the sharing of varied activities, so giving handicapped people the necessary confidence to take their full place in the community alongside their able-bodied peers. The training of club leaders is an important aspect of PHAB's work and courses are arranged in different parts of the country. In addition to supporting and developing clubs and groups, PHAB arranges residential holiday courses in this country and abroad for people of all ages and for families.

Photography for the Disabled
190 Secrett House, Ham Close, Ham, Richmond, Surrey.
01 948 2342

Possum Users Association
14 Greenvale Drive, Timsbury, Nr. Bath, Avon.
0761 71184
Assists users of Possum equipment. It is run on a voluntary basis by severely disabled people who themselves use Possum, and is dedicated to the financial and social improvement of conditions of its members and other disabled people. Publishes a magazine 'Possability". The Association now has a qualified, full-time welfare officer who will assist disabled people and recommend exactly what equipment he considers appropriate to their needs. He is supported by seven part-time welfare assistants in various parts of the country.

Queen Elizabeth's Foundation for the Disabled
Leatherhead, Surrey, KT2 0BN.
037 284 2204
Comprises four units which provide assessment, further education, vocational training, residential sheltered work, holidays and convalescence for many hundreds of disabled men, women and young people.

Rehabilitation Engineering Movement Advisory Panels (REMAP)
Thames House North, Millbank, London SW1P 4QG.
01 834 4444 - Extension 4112 Mr. Marshall

Rehabilitation Engineering Movement Advisory Panels (REMAP) Scotland
Maulside Lodge, Beith, Ayrshire, KA15 1JJ.
029 483 2566

Riding for the Disabled Association
Avenue R, National Agricultural Centre, Kenilworth, Warwicks.
0203 56107

The Royal Association for Disability and Rehabilitation (RADAR)
25 Mortimer Street, London W1N 8AB
01 637 5400
RADAR acts as a co-ordinating body for the voluntary groups serving
disabled people and is able to provide information on relevant subjects.
It seeks generally to investigate the causes and problems of disablement
and promote measures to eliminate or alleviate them. It is particularly
active in promoting better access to public buildings and has published a
number of Access Guides. Produces a helpful publications list, a first-class
holiday guide, a quarterly journal 'Contact' and a monthly 'Bulletin'.

Scottish Council on Disability
Princess House, Shandwick Place, Edinburgh EH2 4RG.
031 229 8632
Provides a means of consultation and joint action among voluntary and
statutory organisations in Scotland on such topics as employment, acces-
sibility, accommodation, research and volunteer training. Operates an
information service (Scottish Information Service for the Disabled) and
mobile aids centre.

Scottish Trust for the Physically Disabled Limited
9 Wheatfield Road, Edinburgh EH11 2PX.
031 443 5634
The primary object of the Trust is the establishment of facilities in groups
of specially built houses, under the general supervision of wardens, to
enable those who are physically handicapped to lead as nearly normal a
life as possible. It also promotes and funds research in the field of
disability.

Share Community Limited
170 Kingston Road, London SW19
01 542 6241
Sponsors schemes to promote self-help for handicapped people.

Sheltered Housing Assistance for the Disabled (SHAD)
66 Belleville Road, London SW11 6PP.

Spinal Injuries Association (SIA)
5 Crowndale Road, London NW1
01 388 6840
The SIA is a self-help organisation for paraplegics and tetraplegics (spinal
cord injured) which aims to help individuals achieve their own goals,
bring about the best medical care and rehabilitation and stimulate scientific research into paraplegia. The SIA provides information on all aspects
of paraplegia to spinal cord injured, their families and everyone concerned
with their welfare. It motivates members to set and meet objectives in
such areas as home adaptations, wheelchair living, education, self-help
aids and personal care. It offers a form of peer counselling through the
Link Scheme. It seeks to develop communication between statutory and

voluntary bodies on mobility, access, employment, integration and other problems common to all disability groups. It is consulted by government and has advised on the design of new spinal units. It has published 'Able to Work' and booklets on the treatment and care of patients with spinal lesions. It produces a quarterly newsletter and the book 'So You're Paralysed...' by Bernadette Fallon at £2.50 plus 50p postage. Membership is open to all.

Association to Aid Sexual and Personal Relationships of the Disabled (SPOD)
The Diorama, 14 Peto Place, London NW1 4PT.
01 486 9823
SPOD was set up in 1972 by the National Fund for Research into Crippling Diseases, with the object at that time of studying and advising on sexual problems, as might be experienced by disabled people. SPOD's first three years of existence were taken up by intensive research into the sexual aspects of disability. The research was carried out by Bill Stewart, SPOD's first Development Officer. SPOD is now an independent organisation and in a few years it has achieved a great deal with regard to changing peoples' attitudes by bringing discussion into the open and showing that disability doesn't rule out sexual feelings, sexual needs, or, usually, sexual capabilities. At the time of the initial research SPOD showed that the outlook of both the public and professional workers amounted to a denial of sexuality among severely disabled people and a view of them as sexless or sexually inconsiderable. Many of these attitudes still remain, but at least they are changing, and an understanding and tolerance is emerging which is both more healthy for handicapped people themselves and for those who hold such bigoted views. In addition, SPOD is able to advise and counsel individual disabled people by correspondence and, where needed, in their own home areas. Lastly, but very importantly, SPOD arranges a number of educational and training measures on the sexual aspects of disability and will provide speakers for meetings when requested.

Sports Association for People with Mental Handicaps (UK)
c/o The Sports Council, 16 Upper Woburn Place, London WC18 02P.
01 388 1277

Students, National Bureau for Handicapped,
40 Brunswick Square, London WC1.
01 278 3459/3450

Union of the Physically Impaired
Flat 2, St. Giles Court, Dane Road, Ealing, London W13.
01 579 9679

Wales Council for the Disabled
Llys Ifor, Crescent Road, Caerphilly, Mid-Glamorgan CF8 1XL.
0222 869224

Wessex Rehabilitation Association
General Hospital, Tremona Road, Southampton SO9 4XY.
0703 777222

Appendix 2

Helpful Publications

So You're Paralysed
Fallon, Spinal Injuries Association
Written for the newly paralysed person. Down to earth, clear, positive.

Able to Work
Fallon, Spinal Injuries Association
A guide to employment and training. Thorough but beginning to date in parts.

Care Book 1 - Nursing Management in the first 48 Hours Following Injury
Fallon, Spinal Injuries Association
Written for professionals

Paraplegia
Rogers, Faber
Written by a tetraplegic. Thorough, but emphasis rather on the medical approach.

Spinal Cord Injuries
Guttman, Blackwell
The established "bible". Written for doctors.

Spinal Cord Injuries - Psychological Social and Vocational Adjustment
Roberta Trieschmann, Pergamon
The new "bible" written for professionals but of great interest to the alert spinal cord injured person too — explodes a few myths about rehabilitation.

My Second Twenty Years
Brickner, Basic Books
An autobiography, with emphasis on sex and personal relationships.

Tetraplegia and Paraplegia
Bromley, Churchill Livingstone
Written by a physio for other physios. Has good clear explanations, lots of pictures.

The Sexual Side of Handicap: A Guide for the Caring Professions
Bill Stewart, Woodhead Faulkner Ltd.
Intended for members of the caring professions, also useful to voluntary workers and disabled people.

Sexual Options for Paraplegics and Quadriplegics
Mooney, Cole & Chilgren, Quest Publishing Agency
Written by a spinal cord injured person and two doctors experienced in human sexuality research and rehabilitation

Directory for the Disabled
Darnborough & Kinrade, Woodhead Faulkner Ltd.
The best in general advice books. Comprehensive and up to date.

Options — SCI and the Future
Corbett, NSCIF (USA)
A happy book full of success stories — lots of pictures, optimism.

Appendix 3

'Wheelabout '81'

The following comprised the Project Team:

Co-ordinator and Secretary: Mike Mills
Representing Petersfield Lions Club: Bob Chambers
Press and Publicity: David Glanz

Roadcrew: Neil Slatter
           Toni Rickwood
           Bob Slatter
           Eileen Slatter
           Robert Slatter
           Hilda Slatter
           Graham Slatter
           Emma Slatter
           Leah Dance
           John Upfold
           Tizz Taylor-Stoakes
           Dave Futcher
           Dave Harbottle
           Steven Rickwood
           Candy Atherton
           Robert Watts
           Jock Trodden
           Gwyn Smith
           Mike Wally
           Mark Walker
           Hugh Carter
           Phil Brompton

Mark Walsh, a fellow tetraplegic, volunteered to stand in for
Neil in the event of accident or incapacity.